gorgeous suppers

Annie Bell was a chef before becoming a full-time food writer and author. She has written for *Vogue*, the *Independent*, and *Country Living*, and is now the principal cookery writer for *The Mail on Sunday*'s YOU magazine. Her books include *Evergreen*, which was shortlisted for the André Simon and Glenfiddich Food Writing awards; and more recently, *Soup Glorious Soup* and *The Camping Cookbook*. Annie is also the author of *Gorgeous Puddings*, *Gorgeous Cakes*, *Gorgeous Greens* and *Gorgeous Christmas*.

Annie Bell's

gorgeoussuppers

with photographs by Chris Alack

Vincent Square Books

This edition published in 2011 by
Vincent Square Books, an imprint of Kyle Books
23 Howland Street
London W1T 4AY
www.kylebooks.com

First published in Great Britain in 2008 by
Kyle Cathie Limited

ISBN 978-0-85783-040-1

A CIP catalogue record for this title is available from the British Library.

Annie Bell is hereby identified as the author of this work in accordance with Section 77 of
the Copyright, Designs & Patents Act 1988.

Editor: Suzanna de Jong
Design: pinkstripedesign@hotmail.com
Copy Editor: Annie Lee
Proofreader: Stephanie Evans
Indexer: Anna Norman
Photographer: Chris Alack
Home Economist: Clare Lewis
Prop Stylist: Sue Radcliffe
Production: Sha Huxtable
Colour reproduction: Colourscan, Singapore
Printed in China by C&C Offset Printing Co., Ltd.

contents

introduction

On any ordinary day, supper is the great treat. I confess to having given up breakfast many years ago, and lunch too is frequently a flimsy grabbed little something eaten in a space between two tasks, and afforded the minimum of time. But supper marks the end of the day and of work; it is a change into another gear, one of relaxation. I love everything about supper, from anticipating what it will be earlier during the day to the start of preparation, which is one of the most relaxing bits. I usually switch on the telly, catch up with the news and settle to a little chopping. And then comes the final sigh of relief as you sit down at the table to chat and exchange news with

your nearest and dearest. Though frankly it doesn't matter if it's only the cat, since going through the whole process is cathartic in itself.

I am assuming here a typical working day, which differs for all of us depending on what we do and whether we have families, and of course their ages. But there is a fair chance the day will seem overcrowded, and there will be a sense of relief at the close of play. And in this way, while supper is a reward, it is also constrained by the practicality of what we actually have time to cook. Anything that leaves us feeling more stressed than when we started will have failed in its potential to soothe.

I have never seen supper in terms of 'Thirty Minute Meals', in the way they are often presented to lure us in, that is, half an hour's preparation prior to eating. I don't think supper can be boxed into a corner; life is too varied for that. And the recipes here make no such claims; some are quicker than others. It is the pattern of the day that is at stake here. More and more of us are based at home or will spend part of the week working from home, so the landscape of what is practical is changing.

I find if I have just put in a couple of hours of concentration at my computer, come teatime I will be hunting round for something to do for twenty minutes in order to get a break. This makes dishes such as casseroles ideal, a little in the way of preparation followed by a couple of hours simmering. If you are going to a drinks party early evening, however, or to see a film, you might want to prepare something earlier in the day to be at the ready for when you arrive home, when a plate of chicken liver pâté with griddled sourdough bread, some chutney and gherkins is just the ticket. Equally, though, you might walk through the door at midnight feeling ravenous, when the only thing that will do is a plate of spaghetti puttanesca. My ideal repertoire isn't so much governed by a stopwatch as a 'wardrobe' of dishes that will cover all eventualities.

If anything, this is a collection of recipes bound by mood, veering in the direction of comfort – they are homely, down to earth and delicious. They are also hearty – I rarely go to the trouble of more than one course on an average day. It's as much as any of us can find in the way of time mid-week to cook up a main course. A bowl of thick red homemade tomato soup, or a Spanish omelette laced with olives, calls for little more than a loaf of bread or some slabs of toast in addition.

There are of course occasions when you want to turn supper into more of an event, if friends or relations are dropping round, something that makes a little bit more of a splash than the one hearty course you might normally settle for. My answer to this conundrum is to begin and end with a 'happy marriage'. That is, a couple of ingredients that require virtually zero preparation but that bring out the best in each other, such as a plate of fine smoked salmon draped casually to one side of a large platter with some slivers of avocado on the other side. Add a grinding of black pepper, a few lemon wedges and a loaf of brown soda bread into the equation and you're there. While for pud it could be a big bar of Valrhona chocolate and some muscatel raisins with a small glass of sweet wine. All of which are sufficiently luxurious to set the endorphins flowing.

beginnings six notes to start on

salmon roe and quail's eggs

Two deli luxuries that are effortlessly chic in each other's company. Most simply you could serve a bowl of quail's eggs (boiled for 2½ minutes) with a small jar of salmon roe to dip into. Or spread cocktail blinis (warmed in the oven for 5 minutes) with your faux caviar, squeeze over a little lemon juice and scatter with chopped fresh chives or a dab of sour cream, to hand round with drinks.

smoked salmon with avocado

You want the best smoked salmon you can lay your hands on and meltingly ripe avocados, skinned and cut into quarters. Drape and pile them any way, the bigger the platter the better, then get out your pepper mill and quarter a few lemons.

parma ham with figs and melon

Slivers of scented orange-fleshed Charentais or Cantaloup melon and halved tulip-black figs are sublime draped with wafer-thin rashers of Parma or other air-dried ham such as the suberb Spanish Iberico ham. And it doesn't have to spell all things Seventies – presentation is all. Cut the skin off your melon, halve and scoop out the seeds and slice into slim wedges. Arrange these in a pile on a large plate with fig halves to match, and enough ham to partner, draped loosely into folds.

pâté and cocktail gherkins

One, two, three does it here. Amass a selection of pâtés: a smooth silky chicken liver, a coarse duck with pistachio and perhaps a rabbit terrine or one with snippets of apple. Serve with crisp vegetables cut fine – slivers of carrot and celery heart, breakfast radishes, some cocktail gherkins and silverskin onions, and thick slices of toasted sourdough bread.

parmesan and olives

My husband forever gets into trouble when I go to the fridge to grate some of the big chunk of Parmesan I bought as a standby for a spaghetti supper, only to find it's gone. It's even better thinly shaved and eaten with a drink before dinner than in a risotto or other such. Throw in a few bowls of different kinds of olive, some slow-roasted tomatoes and pickled chillies, and your appetiser is complete. This is also the place for a whole salami, papery skin intact, with a serrated knife to hack away at it.

smoked cod's roe and watercress

Thin slivers of iodine-rich smoked cod's roe with a bunch of peppery watercress, some feisty white bread and unsalted butter is a real treat to savour. But this tawny-hued delicacy is not an ingredient to take prisoners, and most wine tastes filthy in its company, so you want a bottle of ice-frosted lemon vodka to sip from shot glasses.

soups

A famed hostess once rather haughtily remarked that she would never dream of founding a meal on a pond. It has always stuck in my mind and I am inclined to agree. I love soup, and can happily live off it for days on end, not least when I am feeling in need of some kind of inner comfort. It strokes and nurtures, and restores in the subtlest of ways. But I would much rather it formed the focus of supper than was served as an introduction. There is a small aside to this, one that our hostess would approve of, soup shots served in little glasses that sit neatly side by side with puff pastry appetisers as an *amuse-gueule*, but that is the stuff of organised occasions.

Where supper is concerned, soup is for supping by the large bowlful, and, assuming you have room, a second one too. So the most that is called for is a selection of cheeses and a green salad to follow. This makes it one of the most practical of suppers too, as there are very few soups that take more than fifteen minutes' chopping followed by a spell of simmering on the hob.

It is the classics that tend to make up my favourites, such as a really good homemade tomato soup in imitation of Heinz, especially when dished up with mini rarebits. Lentil too has the power to restore in a way that is unique, while a bowl of French onion soup with a shared bottle of wine can be more attractive than traipsing to the local bistro on a cold January evening. And at the end of a dusty scorcher, I can put money on it that if I give my husband a vote on what he most feels like eating, he'll say a bowl of gazpacho. Latterly I have taken to making this as a lightly set jelly in ramekins, when it can be eaten with slivers of smoked salmon or morsels of lobster. And then there's white gazpacho, which is as fast to throw together as a smoothie, and slips down just as easily.

This is the great hero of our childhood, and I still turn to a tin of Heinz in times of trouble, such as having flu or a cold, when it conjures immeasurable comfort. Though if I am honest, as an adult too often I feel disappointed by its blandness and want to jazz it up. Still, it's up there on its pedestal, and its character is central to the perfect tomato soup.

For the very best, treat yourself to cherry tomatoes on the vine, which are the sweetest and most intensely flavoured of all. But the real secret here is celery salt, an old-fashioned spice that works wonders for Bloody Marys, and failing that you could sauté a couple of sliced sticks of celery heart with the onions. Some little rarebits will make gorgeous asides.

best-ever tomato soup

50g unsalted butter

2 onions, peeled and chopped

4 garlic cloves, peeled
   and finely chopped

1.5kg plum tomatoes, coarsely chopped

150ml whipping cream

¾ teaspoon caster sugar

sea salt

cayenne pepper

celery salt

Serves 6

Melt the butter in a large saucepan over a lowish heat and cook the onion for about 10 minutes until lightly coloured, stirring occasionally and adding the garlic a couple of minutes before the end. Add the tomatoes and give them a stir, then cover the pan with a lid and cook for 20–25 minutes, stirring halfway through, until they are soft and soupy.

Purée the tomatoes in a liquidiser and pass through a sieve. Return them to a clean pan, add the cream, sugar and just a little salt, and gently simmer for 15 minutes. Season with cayenne pepper and celery salt to taste.

on the side
little rarebits

6 slices day-old white bread

Rarebit Mixture

30g day-old white bread (excluding
   crusts)

250g mature Cheddar, cut into
   chunks

30g unsalted butter

3 tablespoons stout

1 teaspoon Dijon mustard

1 teaspoon Worcestershire sauce

1 medium organic egg

Place the bread for the rarebit mixture in the bowl of a food processor and whiz to crumbs. Add all the remaining ingredients for the mixture and blend to a paste. You can make this well in advance, in which case transfer it to a bowl, cover and chill it.

Toast the 6 slices of bread, cut into triangles or smaller pieces, leaving the crusts on, and thickly spread with the rarebit mixture. You need to grill them under a lowish grill to cook the inside of the mixture, either under a medium heat for 5–7 minutes, or a low heat for about 5 minutes, turning it up to brown the top. Serve with the soup – you could float them in it too.

However sweet your peas, they will seem even more so in the company of bacon, here served as crisply grilled thin rashers. It's becoming almost as frequent to come across shelled fresh peas as frozen, and when you need this many of them it's a convenience to exploit. But make sure they are still a fresh grass-green; once they start fading or threatening to sprout they will have lost their charm.

fresh pea soup with bacon sticks

Soup

25g unsalted butter
1 onion, peeled and chopped
150ml white wine
600g fresh shelled peas
750ml chicken stock (see page 31)
sea salt, black pepper
1 teaspoon caster sugar
10 good-sized fresh basil leaves
chopped fresh flat-leaf parsley to serve

Bacon Sticks

8 rashers of unsmoked streaky bacon,
  cut into 2 long strips lengthwise

Serves 4

Melt the butter in a large saucepan over a medium heat, add the onion, and cook for several minutes until it is translucent and soft. Add the wine and cook until it is syrupy. Add the peas and stir, then add the stock, seasoning and sugar. Bring to the boil over a high heat and simmer for 2–3 minutes.

In the meantime heat the grill and lay the bacon strips out on the grid of a grill pan. Grill until golden and crisp on both sides. Pile on to a plate.

Place the soup in a food processor with the basil leaves and purée, then adjust the seasoning – it may well need more salt. I like a slight texture to this soup, but if you prefer it completely smooth you can liquidise it in a blender, and if necessary pass it through a sieve. Return to the saucepan, rewarm and serve scattered with parsley, accompanied by the bacon sticks.

The browning of the onions is everything here – after a brief simmer in a good chicken broth they cast their golden caramelisation into the soup. That and a slug of brandy at the end make this as warming as it looks, with its sizzling Gruyère croûtons in the middle.

french onion soup

50g unsalted butter
3 onions, peeled, halved and
   thinly sliced
150ml white wine
900ml chicken stock (see page 31)
sea salt, black pepper
2 tablespoons brandy
4 slices of baguette, toasted
75g grated Gruyère

Serves 4

Melt the butter in a large saucepan over a medium heat and cook the onions gently for 20–30 minutes until they are a deep even gold, stirring frequently. It's really important to take your time here and not rush it. Add the wine and simmer until well reduced, then add the stock and some seasoning, bring to the boil and simmer over a low heat for 10 minutes. Stir in the brandy.

Preheat the grill and ladle the hot soup into 4 deep soup bowls. Float a slice of baguette in the centre of each one, scatter the cheese over the slice and grill until golden and bubbling.

This simple broccoli soup derives from the chef Jean-Christophe Novelli, who in turn garnered it from his mother, a great traditional cook he says; it has often featured on his menus.

broccoli soup
with roquefort croûtons

Soup

400g broccoli, stalks trimmed
1.2 litres chicken stock (see page 31)
sea salt, black pepper
1 Spanish onion, peeled, halved
   and sliced
150g maincrop potatoes, peeled
   and diced
175g crème fraîche

Croûtons

100g Roquefort
8 x 1cm slices of day-old baguette,
   toasted

Serves 4

Thickly slice the broccoli stalks and divide the florets. Bring the stock to the boil in a medium-size saucepan with some salt and pepper and add all the vegetables. Bring back to the boil, cover and cook over a low heat for 15 minutes. Pass the soup through a mouli-légumes into a bowl, add the crème fraîche, and once this has melted taste for seasoning, bearing in mind that Roquefort is salty and will season it further.

Heat the oven to 220°C fan/240°C/gas mark 9 or as high as it will go. Transfer the soup to a large cast-iron casserole and bring it to a simmer on top of the stove. Slice the Roquefort thinly and lay it on the slices of toasted baguette. Float these on the surface of the soup and place the casserole in the hot oven for 5 minutes, uncovered, until the cheese is melted and bubbling. Ladle the soup and croûtons into warm bowls and serve straight away.

This is arguably my favourite oriental soup – chicken with coconut is always a winner, here backed up by that quintessential trio, chilli, garlic and ginger. You could pad it out with some cooked rice too.

coconut and chicken soup

2 garlic cloves, peeled
1 teaspoon chopped fresh
  medium-hot red chilli
2cm piece of fresh ginger, peeled
  and coarsely chopped
2 tablespoons groundnut oil
3 shallots, peeled and finely
  sliced
2 medium carrots, trimmed,
peeled and finely sliced
1 x 400ml tin of coconut milk
600ml chicken stock (see page
  31)
2 chicken breasts, skinned
2 tablespoons fish sauce
a couple of squeezes of lemon
  or lime juice
½ teaspoon caster sugar
2 spring onions, trimmed and
  finely sliced
fresh coriander leaves to serve

Serves 4

Place the garlic, chilli and ginger in a small blender such as a coffee grinder and reduce to a paste. Heat the oil in a medium-size saucepan over a medium heat, add the paste and fry it momentarily, then add the shallots and carrots and fry for a couple of minutes, stirring frequently, until nice and glossy. Pour in the coconut milk and the stock, bring to the boil and simmer over a low heat for 10 minutes.

Cut out and discard the white tendon on the underside of each chicken breast and thinly slice them across. Add the chicken to the soup and simmer for another 2 minutes. Stir in the fish sauce, the lemon or lime juice and the sugar. Ladle the soup into small deep bowls, with the chicken and vegetables in the centre, and scatter over some spring onion and coriander.

Lentil soup is more in the way of 'mother love' that we could happily exist on in times of trouble; little seems to nurture more adeptly. This particular one uses both the meaty, pale green Continental lentils and the pert little Puy lentils that keep their shape. A flurry of Parmesan also goes to elevate it beyond its hippy roots.

lentil and lemon soup

10 tablespoons extra virgin olive oil

4 carrots, trimmed, peeled and sliced

1 celery heart, trimmed and sliced

2 onions, peeled and chopped

6 garlic cloves, peeled and finely chopped

200g Continental green lentils, rinsed

1 bay leaf

2 strips of lemon zest, removed with
   a potato peeler

a pinch of dried chilli flakes

2 litres chicken stock (see page 31)

sea salt

150g Puy lentils

2 tablespoons lemon juice

freshly grated or shaved Parmesan to serve

Serves 6

Heat 4 tablespoons of olive oil in a large saucepan over a medium heat, add the carrot, celery and onion, and cook, stirring occasionally, for 10–15 minutes until soft and starting to colour. Stir in the garlic and cook for a few minutes longer. Stir in the Continental lentils, and add the bay leaf, lemon zest and chilli. Pour in the stock and season with salt, bring to the boil and simmer over a low heat for 35–45 minutes or until the lentils are tender.

At the same time, bring a medium-size pan of water to the boil, add the Puy lentils and simmer for 20–30 minutes until tender. Drain them into a sieve, return them to the pan and toss with the remaining oil, the lemon juice and some salt.

Discard the bay leaf and zest, then liquidise the soup in batches and taste it for seasoning. Serve with the dressed lentils spooned in the centre, scattered with Parmesan.

This is a real winter-time Sunday night soup in our house, post-roast when there's a pan of chicken stock on the hob, and various odds and ends of root vegetables in the basket. It's also a first call in the days after Christmas, when all you need is some blue cheese and walnuts to crack for afters.

lentil, potato and rosemary broth

4 tablespoons extra virgin olive oil
2 leeks, trimmed and sliced
3 large carrots (approx. 350g),
  peeled and cut into 1cm dice
5 small turnips (approx. 350g),
  peeled and cut into 1cm dice
4 x 5cm sprigs of fresh rosemary
200ml white wine
1.8 litres chicken stock (see page
  31) or turkey stock
600g maincrop potatoes, peeled
  and cut into 1cm dice
150g Continental green or Puy lentils
1 small dried chilli, finely chopped
sea salt

Serves 6

Heat the olive oil in a large saucepan over a medium heat, add the leeks, carrots, turnips and rosemary and cook for about 8 minutes until glossy and beginning to soften. Add the wine and cook to reduce it by half. Add the stock, potatoes, lentils and dried chilli, bring to a simmer, then cover and cook over a low heat for 40 minutes. Season generously with sea salt about 10 minutes before the end. Give it a good stir, taste for seasoning and ladle into warm bowls.

This hovers on the fine dividing line between a soup and a stew that you can ladle over a slice of toasted coarse-textured white or sourdough bread, rubbed with garlic and drizzled with olive oil. Some thick slices of chorizo in there would turn it into an even heartier bowlful.

a hearty squash soup

extra virgin olive oil
1 large onion, peeled and
   finely chopped
4 celery sticks, trimmed and
   thickly sliced
4 tomatoes
3 garlic cloves, peeled and
   finely chopped
¾ teaspoon ground cumin
¾ teaspoon ground coriander
a pinch of saffron filaments (about 20)
a pinch of dried chilli flakes
2 butternut squash (approx. 800g
   each), skin and seeds removed,
   thickly sliced
1.2 litres chicken stock (see page 31)
sea salt, black pepper
1 x 400g tin of chickpeas, drained
   and rinsed
150g baby spinach leaves

Serves 6

Heat 4 tablespoons of olive oil in a large saucepan over a medium heat. Add the onion and celery and fry for about 10 minutes until lightly coloured, stirring occasionally. In the meantime, bring a small pan of water to the boil. Cut out a cone from the top of each tomato, dunk them into the water for about 20 seconds, then transfer them to a bowl of cold water. Slip off the skins and coarsely chop the tomatoes.

Add the garlic, spices and chilli flakes to the pan, stir for a moment until nice and fragrant, then add the squash and stir to coat it in the oil. Add the tomatoes, the stock and some seasoning, bring to the boil and simmer for 20 minutes. Coarsely mash the squash using a potato masher and taste for seasoning. Stir in the chickpeas and spinach and simmer for a couple of minutes longer. Serve in warm bowls, with some olive oil poured over.

Mushrooms are so replete with juices, they make excellent soups, and any variety will do here, though the combination of chestnut and shiitake is particularly good. Unless one is out there picking in the forest it's hard to run to wild, but these two make a good semblance.

double mushroom soup

Soup

extra virgin olive oil

30g unsalted butter

100g unsmoked rindless streaky bacon, diced

4 shallots, peeled, halved and sliced

1 tablespoon fresh rosemary leaves

3 garlic cloves, peeled and finely chopped

1 maincrop potato (about 200g),
   peeled and diced

100ml white wine

400g chestnut mushrooms, trimmed
   and sliced

200g shiitake mushrooms, trimmed and sliced

800ml chicken stock (see page 31) or
   vegetable stock

¼ teaspoon dried chilli flakes

sea salt

On Top

130g shiitake mushrooms, trimmed and sliced

coarsely chopped fresh flat-leaf parsley

Serves 4

Heat a tablespoon of oil and the butter in a large saucepan over a medium heat, add the bacon and fry for 4–5 minutes until starting to colour. Add the shallots and rosemary and fry for about another 3 minutes, stirring in the garlic just before the end. Stir in the potato, then add the wine and simmer until well reduced and syrupy.

Heat a tablespoon of oil in a large frying pan over a high heat, add about a third of the mushrooms and fry for a few minutes, stirring frequently, until golden. Remove and cook the remainder in the same fashion. Add the fried mushrooms to the saucepan, then add the stock, chilli and some salt, bring to the boil and simmer for 10 minutes. Whiz the soup in batches in a food processor.

To serve, heat a tablespoon of oil in a large frying pan, add the 130g of shiitake mushrooms, season with salt and sauté for several minutes until softened and golden. Ladle the soup into warm bowls, scatter the mushrooms over, then plenty of parsley, and drizzle with a little oil.

I've lost count of the times I have made this soup, sometimes with rocket but often with watercress too, which grows wild in our stream. It is simply one of the most nurturing and delicious soups there are, and without calling on a blender or food processor is amenable to being made in small quantities. A word on the chicken stock though: this should be fresh and homemade, certainly a good quality.

rocket and potato soup

50g unsalted butter
4 medium onions, peeled and
   chopped quite finely
225ml white wine
700g potatoes, peeled and sliced
1.2 litres chicken stock (see page 31)
sea salt, black pepper
200g rocket, stalks trimmed
crème fraîche to serve

Serves 4–6

Melt the butter in a large saucepan over a medium-low heat, add the onions and cook for 6–7 minutes until soft and glossy, without colouring. Add the wine, turn the heat up, bring to the boil and reduce by two-thirds. Next, add the potatoes, the stock and some seasoning and bring back to the boil, then turn the heat back down again and simmer for 15 minutes, or until the potatoes are tender when pierced with a knife. Using a potato masher, coarsely mash the potatoes into the soup. It needn't be completely smooth, small nibs of tattie are welcome. You can prepare the soup to this point in advance.

Just before eating, thinly slice the rocket, reserving a few small leaves to serve. Add the sliced rocket to the pan, bring back to the boil and taste for seasoning. Ladle into warm soup bowls with a teaspoon of crème fraîche in the centre. Top with the reserved rocket leaves and serve straight away.

While something approximating Heinz might do it for a hot soup, gazpacho is the ultimate chilled tomato soup, and lends itself with panache to being jellied and draped with smoked salmon or a spoonful of salmon roe. You could also serve crisp slivers of toast alongside for scooping it up.

jellied red gazpacho

Soup

6 Supercook gelatine sheets,
  or 1½ x 11g sachets of
  powdered gelatine
1kg small vine tomatoes
1 cucumber, peeled and
  chopped

1 garlic clove, peeled
  and chopped
1 shallot, peeled and chopped
250ml olive oil, or 125ml
  extra virgin olive oil plus
  125ml groundnut oil
½ tablespoon red wine or
  sherry vinegar
1 tablespoon golden
  caster sugar
2 rounded teaspoons sea salt
a grinding of black pepper

On Top

125g sliced smoked salmon,
  cut into strips
2 tablespoons crème fraîche
  or fromage frais
1 tablespoon small capers,
  rinsed

Serves 6

It's important that all the ingredients for the soup are at room temperature. If using gelatine sheets, cut them into broad strips, soak them in a bowl of cold water for 5 minutes, and drain. Pour 4 tablespoons of just-boiled water over the gelatine, stir until it dissolves, and leave it to cool to room temperature.

If using powdered gelatine, sprinkle it over about 6 tablespoons of just-boiled water in a small bowl. Leave it for a few minutes, then stir to dissolve. If it hasn't completely dissolved, stand the bowl in another bowl of boiling water, leave it for a few minutes longer, and stir again. Alternatively, set the bowl over a pan with a little simmering water in it and gently heat, stirring. Leave this to cool to room temperature.

In the meantime place all the remaining ingredients for the soup in a blender and reduce to a purée, then pass through a sieve. You will have to do this in batches. Stir a little of the purée into the gelatine, then stir this back into the purée. Divide the soup between six 200–250ml cups, glasses or bowls (or eight 150ml ramekins), cover and chill. Once the jellies begin to set (after an hour or two), give them a stir to make sure they are evenly coloured, then wipe the rims, cover and chill overnight until set.

Serve the jellied soup with a few strips of smoked salmon draped in the centre, a teaspoon of crème fraîche or fromage frais and a few capers scattered over.

This is a Spanish white gazpacho, a beautiful creamy soup that can be whisked together in five minutes and then chilled to cooling perfection for a couple of hours. Traditionally it is served with white grapes, and the sweet and sour nature of pomegranate seeds makes them a delicious alternative.

white gazpacho with pomegranate

150g day-old coarse-textured
    white bread, torn up
300g blanched almonds
3 garlic cloves, peeled and
    coarsely chopped
5 tablespoons extra virgin olive oil
3 tablespoons sherry or
    red wine vinegar
sea salt
750ml cold water
1 pomegranate, seeds removed

Serves 6

Place the bread in a bowl and cover with cold water. Put the almonds into a food processor and whiz for a couple of minutes to a powdered consistency; they should by the end be sticking to the sides of the bowl. Squeeze out the bread, add it to the food processor with the garlic, olive oil, vinegar, 2 teaspoons of salt and a little of the water, and reduce to a creamy purée, scraping down the sides of the bowl as necessary. Slowly pour in the remainder of the water through the funnel with the motor running (depending on the size of your food processor, you may need to transfer the soup to a bowl before you can whisk in the last of the water).

Transfer the soup to a bowl, and taste to check the seasoning – it may benefit from another ½ teaspoon of salt. Cover and chill for a couple of hours, during which time it will thicken a little, to the consistency of single cream.

Serve the soup in bowls, with the pomegranate seeds scattered over.

A long crusty baguette, soaked with butter infused with herbs and garlic, never goes amiss with soup, however retro or Seventies it might feel. We loved it for a reason.

Crisp homemade croûtons are a small touch that will make the most humble soup happy. Both styles of croûton have something going for them. Fried, they are luxuriously rich, while toasted ones are lower in fat and less demanding to make.

herb bread

Blend 50g of softened unsalted butter with 6 tablespoons of chopped soft herbs (a mixture of parsley, chives, chervil and a few leaves of tarragon), a clove of crushed garlic and some seasoning. Slit open a baguette and spread the butter down its length, then wrap it up in foil. Bake for 20 minutes at 180°C fan/200°C/gas mark 6, then open up the foil and cook for another 5 minutes to crisp the crust.

croûtons

fried

groundnut oil for frying
2 large slices of white bread, 1cm thick, crusts removed, diced

Heat about 1cm of groundnut oil in a large frying pan over a medium heat until a cube of bread immersed is immediately surrounded by bubbles. Add half the cubes and fry, tossing now and again, until golden and crisp. Transfer them, using a slotted spoon, to a double thickness of kitchen paper and leave to cool. Cook the remainder likewise.

oil-free

2 large slices of white bread, 1cm thick, crusts removed, diced

Preheat the oven to 180°C fan/200°C/gas mark 6. Lay the bread cubes out in a single layer on a baking tray and toast in the oven for 17–20 minutes, giving them a stir halfway through. Remove the tray and leave them to cool.

A perfectly decent chicken stock can be made with water and the proceeds of the Sunday roast. What matters most is the quality of your bird in the first place – if it doesn't have any flavour then neither will the resulting stock.

Use the recipe below as a basic. You can add any vegetables you choose, such as leeks, carrots, celery and garlic, that are going begging, but if you don't the basic will still do you proud.

chicken stock

1 chicken carcass, post-roast
water
sea salt

Makes approx. 1.2 litres

Place the chicken carcass in a saucepan that will hold it snugly, and cover with water by 2cm. Bring it to the boil and skim off any foam on the surface. Add a good teaspoon of salt and keep at a bare simmer for 1 hour. Strain the stock; if it tastes insipid return it to the pan and reduce it by up to half its volume to concentrate the flavour. Leave it to cool, then skim it, cover and chill. Remove any fat from the surface before using it.

eggs 'n' cheese

Some years back I was invited to take a pilot screen-test for a new television programme, along with a number of others. 'We thought we'd ask everyone to make an omelette,' the producer said, 'given that everyone can.' And my heart sank. Even though I have been cooking for many years, I still find a classic omelette, set and lightly golden on the outside and *baveuse* – damp and runny – within, rolled out of the pan with fluid ease, one of the hardest dishes of all to cook. There's no question of taking your time, or stopping midway to consider whether you are getting it right, it's a rollercoaster, and once you've begun you can't get off until you reach the other end. Omelettes make me panic.

I feel I have to tell you this by way of explaining why there are no recipes for classic omelettes in this chapter. I have spent years trying to find ways around having to cook them. So here you will find frittatas and tortillas – tip the mixture into the frying pan and cook it on the hob for a few minutes before chucking it under a hot grill. And the results? A promise of lacy crisp edges, with cheese, herbs and the like sizzling on the surface. They are as good served cold as hot and will do for a number of people.

But if you really want to impress, go for a quiche Lorraine. While there is method and a certain art, it is not one that calls for any skill. A beautifully made quiche is a dish that is heart-stoppingly good, a really short and buttery pastry rolled suitably thin, filled with the lightest savoury custard and lots in the way of melted cheese. In fact, it is difficult to separate eggs and cheese out, they marry so beautifully together, as in twice-baked goat's cheese soufflés, which anyone can cook. And I really do mean anyone.

This is one of my great stand-bys, especially when at our farmhouse in Normandy, where racks of goat's cheeses from the local market provide the wherewithal. You can spin this out with fine rashers of air-dried ham and salami, some olives, caper berries, gherkins and a coarse-textured white or sourdough bread for dipping into the oil. And, as ever, a big leafy salad, but if time is tight you can forgo the garlic.

roasted garlic and toasted goat's cheese

Garlic

6 large heads of garlic
5 sprigs of fresh thyme
sea salt, black pepper
4 tablespoons extra virgin olive oil
25g unsalted butter

Goat's Cheese

3 semi-mature goat's cheeses, e.g.
   Crottin de Chavignol
1 tablespoon fresh marjoram leaves
   (optional)
3 tablespoons extra virgin olive oil

Serves 6

To roast the garlic, preheat the oven to 140°C fan/160°C/gas mark 2. Cut the top off each head of garlic to reveal the cloves and place in a shallow baking dish. Tuck the sprigs of thyme in here and there, season well, pour over the olive oil and dot with the butter. Cover with foil and cook for 1½–2 hours, basting every so often. Serve warm or at room temperature, cool enough to eat with your fingers.

Turn the oven temperature up to 200°C fan/220°C/gas mark 7. Place the goat's cheeses in a shallow ovenproof dish, scatter over the marjoram leaves if using, and trickle over the oil. Cook for 10–12 minutes, until golden and crusty at the edges. The cheese should retain its shape while being soft and melted inside.

No one needs a fondue set when there is such a thing as cheese baked in its box. This is a lazy but luxurious take on this well-loved alpine classic. Coarsely torn morsels of bread and waxy potatoes make for dunking, with a large plate of Parma ham or salami, and some gherkins in tow. It would also make a worthy recipient for shavings of black truffle. And I would ensure a goodly selection of crudités – thin slivers of carrot and celery heart, cherry tomatoes, radishes and chicory leaves – or follow it with a crisp green salad.

Camembert in its box is the classic here, and if it's been aged in Calvados and is coated in fine breadcrumbs that will crisp as it bakes, so much the better. A Petit Livarot is equally up to the task, as is Pont L'Evêque. But source with care from somewhere that knows how to age a cheese – little is more insipid than an under-ripe Camembert, cooked or uncooked.

One Camembert or Petit Livarot will do for two or three people, and a Pont L'Evêque for three or four. Or even more than that if you're dishing it up as an appetiser. If you're entertaining nothing could be simpler: bake as many cheeses as you need and place them between diners.

box-baked cheese

1 x Petit Livarot (270g),
   Camembert (250g) or Pont
   L'Evêque (400g), in its box
chicory leaves

Preheat the oven to 150°C fan/170°C/gas mark 3. Remove any waxed paper surrounding the cheese, and place it back in its box. Now tie a piece of string around the sides of the box to secure it. Bake a Petit Livarot or Camembert for 25 minutes, and a Pont L'Evêque for 35 minutes. Remove it to the table, take off the wooden lid and then, using a spoon, carefully peel back the surface rind. Now dip in with whatever bread or vegetables you are serving.

I guess this is what happens when you marry British passion for 'cheese 'n' tomato' with Italian technique. It's not quite a frittata, but it's not greasy spoon either. Though, coming down in favour of one or the other, a pile of plain buttered toast on a formica table and a mug of tea seems about right.

open-faced
cheese 'n' tomato omelette

2 plum tomatoes
vegetable oil
6 large eggs
2 tablespoons double cream
sea salt, black pepper
50g grated Gruyère
50g grated Emmental
watercress to serve

Serves 3–4

Bring a small pan of water to the boil, immerse the tomatoes for 20 seconds, then cool them in a bowl of cold water. Slip off the skins and thinly slice them, discarding the ends. Brush the top sides with vegetable oil. Break the eggs into a bowl, discarding two of the whites. Add the cream and some seasoning and whisk. Combine the cheeses in a separate bowl.

Preheat the grill. Heat a little oil in an 18cm frying pan with a heatproof handle, and once it is smoking tip out the excess. Pour in the eggs and scramble rapidly with a fork for about 30 seconds, until a third is set. Cook for another 45–60 seconds, during which time sprinkle over the cheese and lay the tomatoes in an overlapping circle, with a slice in the centre. Season and then place under the grill for about 2 minutes, until the edges of the omelette are puffy and lightly coloured. Serve straight away in wedges, with some watercress on the side.

The herbs here are optional: with or without them you will hopefully arrive at something approximating the famed omelette on which the restaurant La Mère Poulard on Mont Saint Michel in Normandy has based its reputation for so many years, the one by which all others will be judged. Though I doubt they rely on Parmesan to produce that to-die-for golden crust as I do — their crust, they allege, is the result of butter and eggs alone. As they guard their secrets as close to their chest as they do, there is no knowing, but much whisking later I felt happy with this pirate copy. And for those like myself who are fazed by rolling omelettes out of the pan, rest assured that there is no sleight of hand.

faux-poulard omelette

4 medium eggs, separated

sea salt, black pepper

40g freshly grated Parmesan

40g unsalted butter

2 tablespoons finely chopped fresh
flat-leaf parsley

2 tablespoons finely chopped
fresh chives

1 teaspoon finely chopped
fresh tarragon

Serves 2

Heat a 25cm cast-iron or other heavy frying pan over a medium-low heat for 4–5 minutes. In the meantime whisk the egg whites in a large bowl until they are stiff (you can use an electric whisk for this), and whisk the yolks in another large bowl with a pinch of salt and a grinding of black pepper. Fold the egg whites into the yolks in two goes, and then add the Parmesan.

Remove the pan from the heat, add the butter and turn the pan around until it is completely melted. Return the pan to the heat, tip in the omelette mixture and smooth the surface to even it out. Cook the omelette for 4–6 minutes, until the underside is a deep crusty gold and the uncooked surface, if you touch it with the back of your finger, feels lukewarm. In the meantime, combine the herbs in a small bowl. Reserving a quarter of them, scatter the remainder of the herbs over the surface of the omelette.

Use a palette knife to lift the edges of the omelette to see how it's doing. Loosen the omelette around the sides and carefully fold one half over, then slip it on to a large plate. Cut it in half and serve with the remaining herbs scattered over.

Try for young broad beans here, or frozen baby ones that won't require skinning. Anything older will benefit from being slipped from its casing after cooking, something that is actually enjoyable should you be sitting on a terrace in the setting sun with a glass of wine to hand.

broad bean, mint and parmesan frittata

150g podded broad beans
6 medium eggs
1 garlic clove, peeled and crushed
   to a paste
sea salt, black pepper
50g freshly grated Parmesan,
   plus 25g finely sliced

a handful of fresh mint leaves,
   coarsely chopped
150g ricotta, coarsely crumbled
2 tablespoons extra virgin olive oil
4 spring onions, trimmed and
   thinly sliced

Serves 4

Bring a medium-size pan of water to the boil. Add the broad beans and boil for 6–7 minutes until tender if fresh, or 4–5 minutes if frozen, then drain them into a sieve.

Whisk the eggs in a bowl with the garlic and some seasoning, then stir in the grated Parmesan and the chopped mint. Fold in the broad beans and ricotta. Preheat an overhead grill to high, and also heat a 26cm frying pan with a heatproof handle over a medium heat. Add a tablespoon of oil to the pan, tip in the egg and broad bean mixture and fry for 3–4 minutes on the hob. Scatter the Parmesan slices over the top of the omelette, then the spring onions, and drizzle over another tablespoon of oil. Place under the grill for 3–5 minutes, until golden and puffy at the sides and just set in the centre. The frittata can be eaten hot or at room temperature.

A spinach omelette with extras – lots of gooey Taleggio and crisp sheaths of Parma ham on top.

spinach and taleggio frittata

4 tablespoons extra virgin olive oil
3 garlic cloves, peeled and
   finely chopped
500g spinach leaves, washed
   and dried
sea salt, black pepper
4 medium eggs
200g Taleggio, rind removed, sliced
4 slices Parma or other air-dried ham,
   cut into two long strips

Serves 4

You will need to cook the spinach in two batches. Heat a tablespoon of oil in a 26cm frying pan with a heatproof handle over a high heat. Add half the garlic and once this sizzles and is fragrant add about a quarter of the spinach. Toss until this collapses a little then add another quarter of spinach. Season and cook until it has wilted. Transfer the spinach to a sieve and press out as much of the liquid as possible, then transfer it to a bowl and prepare the remaining spinach in the same fashion.

Whisk the eggs in a large bowl, add the spinach and a little more seasoning and stir to amalgamate everything.

Preheat the grill to high, and heat the same frying pan in which you cooked the spinach over a medium heat. Add a tablespoon of oil to the pan, tip in the egg and spinach mixture and cook for 3 minutes. In the meantime, arrange the sliced Taleggio over the surface, and drape the slices of Parma ham on top. Drizzle over a tablespoon of oil and place the pan under the grill for another 3–4 minutes. Serve the frittata hot or at room temperature.

Were it not that my husband ate about five helpings of this, I was thinking of making it a little thinner, but obviously there's something about its depth that keeps you coming back for more.

spanish omelette with olives

extra virgin olive oil
500g medium waxy potatoes,
  peeled or scrubbed, and thickly
  sliced
sea salt, black pepper
3 onions, peeled, halved and
  thinly sliced
6 medium eggs
3 tablespoons coarsely chopped
  fresh flat-leaf parsley
125g black olives, pitted and halved

Serves 6

Heat 2 tablespoons of olive oil in a large frying pan over a medium heat. Add the potatoes and cook them for about 5 minutes, turning them now and again, until they are coated in the oil. Season them with salt, add 150ml of water to the pan, cover it with a large tightly fitting saucepan lid and cook over a low heat for 10–15 minutes, stirring halfway through, until the potatoes are tender when pierced with a knife. Using the lid, drain off any excess water and leave, covered, in the pan until ready to use.

Heat another couple of tablespoons of oil in a large saucepan over a medium heat. Add the onions and cook them gently for 15–20 minutes, until they are nicely golden and silky, stirring them frequently. Season them, transfer to a bowl and leave to cool.

Whisk the eggs with some seasoning in a bowl, then stir in the parsley and olives. Fold in the onions, then the potatoes. Preheat the grill to high, and also heat a 26cm frying pan with a heatproof handle over a medium heat. Add a tablespoon of oil to the pan, tip in the egg and potato mixture, level the surface and cook for 3–4 minutes. Drizzle over another tablespoon of oil and place under the grill, 5–7cm away from the heat, for 4–8 minutes, until golden. There should be a gentle give in the centre to leave it slightly wet if eating it hot; it will firm up if you are eating it cold.

This is take two on a Spanish omelette, that little bit more soignée than a frying pan affair and with it I guess comes a little extra effort. It's one for serving at room temperature, so you can make it well in advance.

tortilla with chorizo

4 tablespoons extra virgin olive oil
1kg medium waxy potatoes, peeled
   and thickly sliced
sea salt, black pepper
5 onions, peeled, halved and sliced
a knob of unsalted butter
75g freshly grated Parmesan
9 medium eggs, whisked
100g thinly sliced chorizo

Serves 6–8

Heat 2 tablespoons of olive oil in a large frying pan over a medium heat. Add the potatoes and cook for about 5 minutes, turning them now and again to coat them in the oil. Season with salt, add 150ml of water to the pan, cover it with a large lid and cook over a low heat for 10–15 minutes, until the potatoes are just tender. Drain off any excess water and leave, covered, to cool.

Heat another couple of tablespoons of oil in a large saucepan over a medium heat, add the onions and cook them gently for about 20 minutes until they are nicely golden and silky, stirring them frequently. Season them, transfer them to a bowl and leave to cool.

Preheat the oven to 180°C fan/200°C/gas mark 6. Use the butter to grease a 20cm, 9cm deep cake tin with a removable base and dust it with a little grated Parmesan. Season the eggs and coat the base of the tin with a few tablespoons of this, then use half of the remainder to coat the potato slices, and mix the rest with the onions. Lay half the potato slices over the base of the tin. Lay half the chorizo slices on top, then the onions, and then the rest of the potato slices. Lay the remaining chorizo on top, scatter over the remaining Parmesan and drizzle over a little oil.

Place the tin on a baking sheet and bake for 45–50 minutes, until golden on the surface and set – it should be no more than slightly wet in the centre when a knife is inserted. Run a knife around the collar of the tortilla and leave it to cool to room temperature. Serve it in wedges.

The ultimately suave take on bacon and eggs that will do you proud whatever the supper. It's probably a little more effort than you will want to go to after a frazzled day at work, but then again maybe not, if you've run up your pastry the evening beforehand. That lightly set custard will certainly soothe any nerves, set with salty snippets of bacon within a warm crumbly shell of pastry. Just gorgeous. The secret is all to do with the ratio of cream to eggs, heavy on the former and light on the latter.

quiche lorraine

250g rindless smoked streaky bacon,
   cut into 1cm dice
1 x 23 x 5cm pre-cooked tart case
   (see opposite)
175g grated Gruyère
300ml whipping cream
150ml milk
3 medium eggs, plus 1 egg yolk
1 teaspoon Dijon mustard
1 teaspoon grainy mustard
freshly ground black pepper

Serves 6

Preheat the oven to 180°C fan/200°C/gas mark 6. Place the bacon in a large frying pan, separating out the pieces. Cook over a very low heat until the fat begins to render, then turn the heat up to medium and continue to cook, stirring frequently, until it begins to colour and crisp. Scatter the bacon over the base of the tart case.

Whisk together all the remaining ingredients, putting half the cheese to one side. There's enough salt in the bacon and cheese to season the tart, and there shouldn't be any need to add extra to the custard mixture, simply some pepper. Pour the custard into the tart case, scatter the reserved cheese over the surface and bake for 35 minutes, or until golden and puffy. Leave the tart to stand for 10 minutes. The quiche is most delicious hot, but also good at room temperature.

shortcrust pastry for a 23cm tart case

Place the flour and salt in the bowl of a food processor, add the butter and reduce to a fine crumb-like consistency. Incorporate the egg yolk, and then, with the motor running, trickle in just enough cold water for the dough to cling together in lumps. Transfer the pastry to a large bowl and bring it together into a ball, using your hands.

Wrap the pastry in clingfilm and chill for at least 1 hour. It will keep well in the fridge for up to a couple of days.

Preheat the oven to 180°C fan/200°C/gas mark 6. Knead the pastry until it is pliable. Thinly roll it out on a lightly floured surface and carefully lift it into a 23cm tart tin with a removable base; it is quite durable and shouldn't tear or collapse. Press it into the corners of the tin and run a rolling pin over the top to trim the edges. Reserve the trimmings to patch the case after it is baked. Prick the base with a fork and line it with a sheet of foil, tucking it over the top to secure the pastry sides to the tin. Now weight it with baking beans – dried pulses will do nicely.

Bake the case for 15 minutes, then remove the foil and baking beans. If any of the sides have shrunk more than they should, use a little of the reserved pastry to patch them, as the tart can only be filled as far as the lowest point of the sides. Brush the base and sides of the case with the reserved egg white, then bake it for another 10 minutes until lightly coloured. This glaze helps to seal the pastry and prevent the custard from soaking in.

225g plain flour
a pinch of sea salt
150g unsalted butter, chilled
   and diced
1 medium egg, separated

tart tins

Given that pastry sometimes shrinks, it is a good idea to start off with a tart tin about 5cm deep. Failing that, you could forgo the crimped edges and use a cake tin with a removable collar – you can always trim the sides after cooking if they seem too deep. But I'd avoid china quiche dishes, as they are rarely deep enough and make it difficult to serve the tart without breaking it.

We're heading for a full English breakfast here, and tempting as it is to add sausages, I think I'd serve them on the side.

bacon, egg and mushroom tart

200g rindless smoked streaky bacon, sliced into 1 cm dice

1 x 23 x 5cm pre-cooked tart case (see page 47)

2 tablespoons groundnut oil

1 shallot, peeled and finely chopped

250g mixture of wild and cultivated mushrooms, trimmed and sliced

175g grated mature Cheddar

300ml whipping cream

150ml milk

3 medium eggs, plus 1 egg yolk

1 scant teaspoon Dijon mustard

black pepper

Serves 6

Preheat the oven to 180°C fan/200°C/gas mark 6. Separate out the pieces of bacon, place them in a large frying pan and cook over a very low heat until the fat begins to render, then turn the heat up to medium and cook, stirring frequently, until the bacon begins to colour and crisp. Scatter the bacon over the base of the tart case.

Discard the bacon fat and add the groundnut oil to the pan, then add the shallot and cook for a moment until it softens. Add the mushrooms, and toss frequently until they are soft and starting to colour. If any liquid is given out in the process, keep cooking until it evaporates. Scatter over the base of the tart case.

Whisk together all the remaining ingredients, putting half the cheese to one side. There's enough salt in the bacon and cheese to season the tart, and shouldn't be any need to add any extra to the custard mixture, simply a grinding of pepper. Pour the custard into the tart case, scatter the reserved cheese over the surface and bake for 35 minutes until golden and puffy. Leave to stand for 20 minutes before serving. This is good eaten hot or at room temperature and can be reheated too.

Spinach combined with any kind of cheese is a wow in a tart – feta doesn't so much melt as soften to a lovely moussey consistency, while the tomatoes take on its saline streak. And it's as good eaten cold as hot.

spinach, feta and tomato tart

450g baby spinach, picked over and washed
400ml whipping cream
2 medium eggs, plus 1 egg yolk
1 tablespoon freshly grated Parmesan
1 garlic clove, peeled and crushed to a paste
sea salt, black pepper

200g feta, cut into 1cm dice
1 x 23 x 5cm pre-cooked tart case (see page 47)
125g cherry tomatoes, halved
vegetable oil

Serves 6

Place the washed spinach in a large saucepan, pressing it down to get it all in. Cover it with a tightly fitting lid and cook over a low heat for 10 minutes, stirring halfway through, by which time it should have wilted and be cooked through. Drain the spinach into a sieve, pressing out as much water as possible. This part is important, otherwise the moisture will seep down into the pastry. Place the spinach on a board and coarsely chop it with a large sharp knife.

Preheat the oven to 180°C fan/200°C/gas mark 6. Whisk together the cream, eggs and yolk, Parmesan, garlic and some seasoning. Mix in the spinach, then gently fold in half the feta. Transfer the spinach filling to the tart case. Toss the halved cherry tomatoes and remaining feta with just enough oil to coat them and scatter over the top of the tart. Grind over some black pepper and bake for 35 minutes, until puffy, golden and set in the centre. Remove the collar from the tart and leave it to cool for 10 minutes. This tart is equally delicious served at room temperature.

These rich little soufflés look and taste divine. There are two takes, depending on whether you're wearing horns or wings. You can either hark back to the Seventies and blow the cholesterol by smothering them with cream when baking them a second time, or make a fresh tomato sauce before you return them to the oven, which is a little more virtuous.

twice-baked goat's cheese soufflés

300ml whole milk
½ onion, peeled
6 cloves
50g salted butter
45g plain flour
1 x 150g mature goat's cheese (e.g.
    Crottin de Chavignol or chèvre log),
    rind removed, crumbled
sea salt, black pepper
2 medium eggs, separated

Serves 6

Heat the oven to 180°C fan/200°C/gas mark 6. Bring the milk to the boil with the onion and cloves in a small saucepan and leave to infuse for 15 minutes. Melt the butter in a small non-stick saucepan, add the flour and cook for a minute or two until floury in appearance. Now strain the milk and gradually, working off the heat, beat it into the flour and butter using a wooden spoon. Return the mixture to a medium heat and cook for several minutes, stirring, until it is really thick and glossy.

Remove from the heat, stir in the crumbled goat's cheese and some seasoning. Let it cool for a few minutes while you stiffly whisk the egg whites in a bowl. Beat the egg yolks into the sauce, and then the egg whites in three goes.

Butter six 150ml ramekins and divide the mixture between them. Place these in a 30 x 20cm roasting dish with boiling water coming halfway up the sides of the ramekins and bake for 15 minutes, until the soufflés are risen and lightly coloured. Remove and leave them to cool in the roasting tin, when they will sink. Run a knife around the edge of the soufflés and gently prise them out, then arrange them back in the roasting dish the right way up, having drained and dried it. The soufflés can be prepared to this point in advance, up to the night before, in which case cover the dish with cling film and chill them.

angel sauce

900g plum tomatoes, halved
sea salt
1 teaspoon caster sugar
40g unsalted butter
4–5 tablespoons extra virgin
   olive oil
3 tablespoons freshly grated
   Parmesan
1 tablespoon oregano leaves

Place the tomatoes in a medium-size pan, cover and gently stew for 20–30 minutes, until soft and mushy, stirring after 5–10 minutes. Press through a mouli-légumes or a sieve into a bowl, then return to the pan and add a teaspoon of salt, the sugar, butter and 3 tablespoons of olive oil. Bring to the boil and simmer over a low heat for 30 minutes, until you have a thin puréed sauce. Pour into a bowl and leave to cool.

To serve, preheat the oven to 200°C fan/220°C/gas mark 7. Pour the tomato sauce over and around the soufflés to a depth of several millimetres (you probably won't need quite all of it). Scatter over the Parmesan and oregano, and drizzle over another tablespoon or two of olive oil. Bake for 20 minutes until they are risen and crusty on the surface, and golden at the edges. Serve straight away.

devil sauce

sea salt, black pepper
300ml double cream
1 tablespoon fresh thyme leaves
3 tablespoons freshly grated
   Parmesan

To serve, preheat the oven to 200°C fan/220°C/gas mark 7. Season and pour the cream over the soufflés, then scatter over the thyme and the Parmesan. Bake for 15 minutes until they are risen and crusty on the surface. Serve straight away.

carbs

There are certain supper times when only a plate of pasta will do, a big Italian hug. Long slippery strands of spaghetti to be sucked from the bowl, elegant tongue-curls of trofie, blowsy shells and silken layers of lasagne. Without wanting to eat it every single day, pasta holds a very particular and special place in our hearts. That said, my children could quite happily live off it, and if I'm very busy they sometimes do, their favourite being sizzling oven-baked gratins, layered with oodles of gooey cheese.

For my husband and me alone, it's likely to be linguine alla carbonara (not least because we always have decent bacon and eggs knocking around). And if we're all eating together it's almost certainly spaghetti puttanesca, for which it is also worth ensuring there are always capers, anchovies and chilli in the house.

Next in importance to sauce is shape. The king obviously is spaghetti, and the longer the better here. The joy of coming across those over-long crinkly paper packets of spaghetti, so central to the Sixties – kitchens of that decade were defined by tall glass jars. And macaroni tastes almost as good, so there's obviously a retro thing going on. Macaroni cheese is a dish I turn to time and time again; the most glamorous and inspired rendition I have eaten was at a bistro in St Tropez, where it came studded with lobster.

Risottos have acquired a new lease of life in my kitchen, ever since I discovered a way of baking them in the oven. Though there are times when the process of hovering around the stove and judging the risotto to be at the right consistency to accept another ladle of simmering stock is just the kind of therapy that's called for after a day at work, and is positively relaxing.

Famously this derives from the slums of Naples, named after those ladies of the night. But more famously in our house it is the one and only pasta dish my husband and son can cook, so it sees many an outing, normally when I feel I've cooked my last and they realise they're unlikely to get fed unless they take to the stove. We nearly always have the necessary to hand, and it is one of the most delicious and convenient spaghetti dishes. And, should the occasion be a last-minute supper when a friend's dropped in, they are unlikely to feel hard done by.

spaghetti puttanesca

400g spaghetti

3 tablespoons extra virgin olive oil

2 garlic cloves, peeled and
  finely chopped

6 salted anchovy fillets, sliced

1 x 400g tin of chopped tomatoes

1 small dried chilli, finely chopped

1 heaped tablespoon capers, rinsed

110g green and black olives,
  pitted and sliced

2 heaped tablespoons chopped
  fresh parsley

sea salt

freshly grated Parmesan to serve
  (optional)

Serves 4

Bring a large pan of salted water to the boil. Add the spaghetti to the pan, stir to separate it and cook until just tender.

At the same time heat the olive oil in a frying pan over a medium heat, add the garlic and anchovies and cook for 1 minute, mashing the anchovies into a paste. Add the tomatoes and the chilli and simmer for about 7 minutes until the sauce is glossy and thickened, stirring occasionally. Stir in the capers, olives and parsley and cook for 1 minute longer.

Drain the pasta, but not too thoroughly, return it to the saucepan, add the sauce and toss. Taste for seasoning and add a little salt if necessary. Serve straight away. I like the tiniest sprinkling of Parmesan, but not too much.

Bacon and eggs pasta — it's not difficult to fathom the appeal of this one, and equally not hard to imagine Anita Ekberg tucking into a plateful after dancing her way round Rome in La Dolce Vita. It's endlessly chic in a Fifties kind of way, which makes it pretty irresistible to some of us.

linguine alla carbonara

1 tablespoon extra virgin
    olive oil
10g unsalted butter
225g unsmoked back bacon,
    rind and fat removed, sliced
    into thin 2–3cm strips
4 tablespoons white wine
450g linguine

3 large eggs
75g freshly grated Parmesan,
    plus extra shavings to serve
3 tablespoons chopped fresh
    flat-leaf parsley
sea salt, black pepper

Serves 4

Place the oil and butter in a frying pan, add the bacon and fry until it turns crisp at the edges. Add the wine and cook for about 1 minute, then remove from the heat.

Bring a large pan of salted water to the boil. Add the linguine, stir to separate it and cook until just tender. Lightly beat the eggs in a large bowl, blend in the Parmesan and the parsley and season well. Drain the pasta, though not too thoroughly, and rapidly toss into the egg and cheese mixture. Quickly reheat the bacon, and toss the entire contents of the pan into the pasta. Taste for seasoning and serve straight away, with more Parmesan scattered on top.

I've been addicted to this combination ever since eating macaroni cheese with lobster at La Table du Marché, Christophe Leroy's brasserie in St Tropez. Langoustines would also go down a treat, but small prawns are that little bit more accessible.

macaroni cheese with prawns

300ml fish stock
150ml white wine
200g small macaroni
350g crème fraîche
100g Beaufort, Comté or
   Gruyère, grated
sea salt, black pepper
250g cooked and shelled prawns
2 tablespoons fresh breadcrumbs
25g unsalted butter

Serves 6

Place the fish stock and wine in a small saucepan, bring to the boil over a medium-high heat and reduce to a small quantity of concentrated liquid. Discard any skin that has formed.

Bring a large pan of salted water to the boil. Add the macaroni and stir to separate it. Cook until just tender, then drain it. While it is cooking, heat the crème fraîche in a small saucepan and simmer vigorously for 4–5 minutes until it thickens slightly, stirring frequently to prevent it from spluttering. Add the reduced stock and the cheese, and stir over a low heat until it melts. Season to taste with salt and pepper.

Preheat the grill. Add the macaroni and the prawns to the sauce and gently warm through, stirring all the time, then tip the mixture into a shallow gratin or other ovenproof dish (I use a 30cm/1.5 litre oval dish). Scatter over the breadcrumbs, dot with the butter and place under the grill until golden and sizzling. There's a lot of spluttering at this point, but don't be bullied into thinking it's done until it's lightly tanned all over. Serve straight away.

Trofie are slender pasta spirals. A speciality of Genoa and hand-rolled by women, no two strands are the same. But any similar design will do – I also have a soft spot for orecchiette.

trofie with sprouting broccoli and pancetta

300g trofie
250g purple sprouting broccoli
   (trimmed weight)
200g rindless unsmoked pancetta
   or streaky bacon, sliced
4 garlic cloves, peeled and
   finely chopped
4 tablespoons white wine
100g freshly grated Parmesan,
   plus extra to serve
sea salt, black pepper

Serves 4

Bring two large pans of salted water to the boil. Add the pasta to one pan, give it a stir and cook for 18–20 minutes, until tender. Cut the broccoli stems and leaves into 1cm lengths, leaving the little heads whole. Add them to the second pan of boiling water and cook at a rolling boil for 2 minutes, then drain into a colander.

Heat the bacon in a large frying pan over a medium heat and fry in the rendered fat for 8–12 minutes until golden and crisp, stirring frequently. Add the garlic 1 minute before the end. Pour in the wine, which will sizzle furiously, and simmer, scraping up all the sticky bits on the bottom of the pan, until reduced by half.

Just before the pasta is ready, reheat the bacon, add the broccoli and heat through. Drain the pasta, reserving half a cup of cooking liquid, and return it to the saucepan. Tip in the contents of the frying pan and toss, then add the Parmesan and the reserved cooking water and stir over a low heat until everything is coated in a creamy emulsion. Season to taste and serve straight away on warm plates, with extra Parmesan at the table.

A butternut squash in the vegetable basket is a great standby. They last almost indefinitely, which makes this pasta dish a regular in our house. And as ever, the pasta shape should be governed by what's in the cupboard – this is just a suggestion.

conchiglie with butternut squash and sage butter

2 butternut squash
   (approx. 800g each)
3 tablespoons extra virgin
   olive oil
sea salt, black pepper
4 garlic cloves, peeled and sliced
300g conchiglie
100g unsalted butter
10g fresh sage leaves
freshly grated Parmesan to serve

Serves 4

Preheat the oven to 180°C fan/200°C/gas mark 6. Cut the skin off the squash, quarter the bulbous part to remove the seeds and slice these sections into wedges. Halve the remaining cylindrical trunks lengthwise and slice 1cm thick. Arrange the squash in a crowded single layer in a baking tray (I use one 38 x 25cm). Drizzle over the olive oil, season and roast for 50–55 minutes, turning the squash after 25 minutes. Scatter the garlic over the squash and give everything another stir 15 minutes before the end.

Halfway through cooking the squash, bring a large pan of salted water to the boil. Add the conchiglie, stir and cook until just tender – most dried varieties take about 10 minutes.

Five minutes before the pasta is due to be ready, melt the butter in a medium-size frying pan over a medium heat. Skim off the surface foam, decant the clarified butter into a bowl and discard the milky residue in the base. Return the clarified butter to the pan and heat, scattering the sage leaves over the surface. Cook until they darken in colour and crisp, then remove from the heat.

Drain the pasta, add it to the roasting pan and gently turn, using a spatula, to coat with the oil and sticky roasting juices. Spoon the butter and sage leaves on top, scatter over some more seasoning and gently toss again. Serve accompanied by the Parmesan.

We are all familiar with a classic lasagne, and most of us love it, not least for all those layers of thin silky pasta. This version is succulent and light, and comes into its own during the summer months. It's also vegetarian.

tomato and basil lasagne

Sauce

1.3kg beefsteak tomatoes
extra virgin olive oil
1 onion, peeled and finely chopped
4 garlic cloves, peeled and
  finely chopped
2 tablespoons tomato purée
75ml red wine
1 bay leaf
2 sprigs of fresh thyme
1 level teaspoon caster sugar
sea salt, black pepper

Lasagne

230–250g yellow or green lasagne
3 x 125g buffalo mozzarellas, drained
  and diced
75g freshly grated Parmesan
8 large basil leaves, torn in half

Serves 6

To skin the tomatoes, bring a large pan of water to the boil. Cut out a cone from the top of each tomato to remove the core, plunge them into the boiling water for 20 seconds and then drop them into a sink of cold water. Slip off the skins and coarsely chop them.

To make the tomato sauce, heat 3 tablespoons of olive oil in a medium-size saucepan over a moderate heat, add the onion and cook for a few minutes until soft and translucent. Add the garlic and stir it around, then add the tomatoes, tomato purée, wine, bay leaf and thyme. Bring to a simmer, and cook over a low heat for 30 minutes, stirring occasionally. Discard the herbs, and beat the sauce to a slushy purée using a wooden spoon. Add the sugar and season with salt and pepper.

Preheat the oven to 180°C fan/200°C/gas mark 6. Select a 28 x 20 x 6cm roasting or baking dish and cover the base with some of the tomato sauce. Then layer the ingredients as follows. First a layer of lasagne; cover this with tomato sauce, scatter over some mozzarella and Parmesan and dot with a couple of the torn basil leaves. Continue with the remaining ingredients, ending with tomato sauce and cheese, omitting the basil from this top layer. You should have 4 layers of pasta in all. Drizzle a tablespoon of olive oil over the surface and cover with foil. You can prepare the lasagne to this point in advance, and chill it for up to 12 hours until you need it. Bake the lasagne for 20 minutes, then remove the foil and bake for another 25 minutes until the top is golden and bubbling. If necessary you can give it a few minutes under the grill. Serve straight away.

Janssen's Temptation goes down in culinary lore as one of the richest and most desirable potato dishes you could dream up – spindly chipped potatoes and slivers of onion baked with a great deal of cream and anchovies that melt into it. This is a more restrained version that won't have you loosening your belt. Serve it with a green salad and there's very little to fret over.

something to tempt janssen

6 maincrop potatoes (approx. 1kg),
   e.g. Maris Piper or Desirée, peeled
   and finely sliced
5 tablespoons extra virgin olive oil
1 garlic clove, peeled and finely
   chopped
sea salt, black pepper
10–15 salted anchovies, chopped
4 tablespoons double cream
50g fresh white breadcrumbs

Serves 6

Preheat the oven to 180°C fan/200°C/gas mark 6. Toss the potatoes in a bowl with 4 tablespoons of extra virgin olive oil, the garlic and a little salt and pepper. Lay them in overlapping slices in a 20 x 30cm gratin dish, or shallow ovenproof dish of an equivalent size, scattering the anchovies over the first couple of layers (you should get about three layers in all). Cover tightly with foil and bake in the oven for 50 minutes, until the potatoes are tender when pierced with a knife.

Turn the oven up to 200°C fan/220°C/gas mark 7, drizzle over the cream, then toss the breadcrumbs with a tablespoon of oil and scatter over. Return the gratin to the oven for 10–15 minutes, until the crumbs are golden. This can be reheated at 200°C fan/220°C/gas mark 7 for 20 minutes.

The French love affair with fondues is almost on a par with that of the Swiss. They have adopted Raclette as their own, the joy of this version being that there is no special paraphernalia involved. All that's demanded is that your diners are seated before the cheese and potatoes come to the table – those moments of gooey perfection are suitably fleeting.

potatoes with raclette and bayonne ham

700g new potatoes, scrubbed or peeled
   as necessary, halved if large
8 slices of Bayonne or other
   air-dried ham
25g gherkins, rinsed and finely
   sliced diagonally
½ red onion, peeled and finely sliced
sea salt, black pepper
250g Raclette (weight excluding rind),
   sliced

Serves 4

Ideally steam the potatoes. Place them in the top half of a steamer set over simmering water in the lower half, cover, and steam for 15–20 minutes, until tender. They could also be boiled if preferred. Towards the end of this time preheat the oven to 200°C fan/220°C/gas mark 7.

Leave the potatoes to cool on a board for about 5 minutes, then slice them. In the meantime arrange the ham on a large plate, and place the gherkins and onion in bowls on the table. Lay the potato slices over the base of a shallow 20 x 30cm gratin or roasting dish, transferring them with a spatula. Season and arrange the cheese on top. Place the gratin in the oven for about 10 minutes, until the cheese is melted and bubbling at the edges; it needn't have coloured. In the meantime be sure your diners are seated and at the ready. Whiz the gratin to the table and serve as quickly as possible while the cheese is lovely and gooey, leaving everyone to help themselves to ham, gherkins and onions.

A friend living in New York first introduced me to this pie, which was doing the rounds of supper parties there at the time. What a great idea, a 'shepherd's pie' base smothered with macaroni cheese – it seems so obvious I wish I'd thought of it first.

macaroni shepherd's pie

Mince

2 tablespoons groundnut oil
3 shallots, peeled and finely chopped
1 large or 2 small carrots, peeled
  and thinly sliced
1 leek, trimmed, halved and
  thinly sliced
2 sticks of celery heart, trimmed
  and thinly sliced
2 sprigs of fresh thyme
750g minced lamb
150ml red wine
2 tablespoons tomato ketchup
1 teaspoon Worcestershire sauce
sea salt, black pepper

Macaroni

35g unsalted butter, plus 15g melted
30g plain flour
750ml whole milk
1 bay leaf
120g mature Cheddar, grated
1 tablespoon Dijon mustard
150g macaroni
2 tablespoons white breadcrumbs
2 tablespoons freshly grated Parmesan

Serves 6

Heat the oil in a large saucepan and cook the vegetables and thyme gently for about 8 minutes over a low heat until glossy and tender, stirring occasionally. Add the minced lamb, turn the heat up, and cook, stirring, until it changes colour and separates. Add the wine, ketchup, Worcestershire sauce and seasoning, bring to a simmer and cook over a low heat for 15 minutes. There should still be some juice – if there appears to be a lot of fat on the surface, skim off the excess. Check the seasoning, then transfer the mince to a shallow ovenproof dish, discarding the thyme (a 20 x 30cm roasting pan allows for plenty of golden surface), and leave to cool for about 20 minutes. You can prepare the pie to this point in advance, cover and chill it until required.

Preheat the oven to 180°C fan/200°C/gas mark 6. Melt the 35g butter for the macaroni in a medium-size non-stick saucepan over a medium heat, add the flour and cook for about 1 minute, until it is seething nicely. Remove from the heat and gradually work in the milk, using a wooden spoon, just a little at a time to begin with. Return this béchamel to the heat and bring to the boil, stirring frequently until it thickens. Add the bay leaf and simmer over a low heat for 10 minutes, stirring occasionally. Remove the bay leaf, stir in the Cheddar and the mustard and taste for seasoning. Bring the sauce back to the boil, stirring. Now liquidise it until really silky.

At the same time as cooking the sauce, bring a medium-size pan of salted water to the boil. Add the macaroni to the pan, give it a stir to separate out the strands and cook until almost tender, leaving it slightly undercooked. Drain the macaroni into a sieve, quite thoroughly, then return it to the pan. Toss the macaroni with the béchamel sauce and pour on top of the mince.

Toss the breadcrumbs and Parmesan with the melted butter and scatter over the pasta. Bake the pie for 25–30 minutes, until the top is golden and sizzling.

Another ode to the Fifties, this time those big jars of salted nuts that used to sit beside the maraschino cherries and Opie's lemon slices in the mirrored drinks cabinet – cashews, macadamias, pecans and peanuts, so good eaten in the company of a cocktail. Any mix will do. This pilaf can be eaten with grilled small cuts – lamb and pork chops, steak or a chicken wing. Some chutney also goes down very well.

cocktail nut pilaf

extra virgin olive oil
1 white onion, peeled, halved and sliced
225g bulgar wheat, rinsed in a sieve
150ml white wine
300ml chicken stock (see page 31)
sea salt, black pepper
4 tablespoons coarsely chopped fresh
   flat-leaf parsley
a squeeze of lemon juice
100g roasted and salted cocktail nuts –
   macadamias, almonds, cashews, brazils,
   pecans, etc.
chutney or salsa to serve

Serves 4

Heat 2 tablespoons of olive oil in a large saucepan over a medium heat. Add the onion and cook gently for 8–10 minutes, stirring occasionally, until it is soft and lightly coloured. Add the bulgar wheat and stir, then pour in the wine and stock and season generously. Bring the liquid to the boil, cover with a tightly fitting lid and cook over a low heat for 10 minutes, by which time all the liquid should have been absorbed. Without removing the lid, turn the heat off and leave it for 15 minutes, during which time it will dry out further and become more tender.

Give the pilaf a stir to fluff up the bulgar wheat, toss in the parsley and season with a squeeze of lemon and more salt if necessary. Serve the pilaf scattered with the nuts. Accompany with whatever chutney or salsa takes your fancy.

A risotto infused with lemon and smothered with caramelised thyme-roasted onions, is, like any other risotto, a tad indulgent with all that Parmesan and butter in there. So just a small green salad to the side might not be a bad idea.

lemon risotto with thyme-roasted onions

Onions

4 red onions, peeled and sliced
  into rounds
8 sprigs of fresh thyme
2 tablespoons extra virgin olive oil
1 tablespoon balsamic vinegar
sea salt, black pepper

Risotto

1.2 litres chicken stock (see page 31)
  or vegetable stock
50g unsalted butter
1 onion, peeled and finely chopped
1 garlic clove, peeled and finely
  chopped
300g risotto rice, e.g. Carnaroli
125ml vermouth
finely grated zest of 2 lemons
2 tablespoons lemon juice
50g freshly grated Parmesan
2 tablespoons double cream
100g Emmental, grated
4 tablespoons finely chopped fresh
  flat-leaf parsley

Serves 4

Preheat the oven to 180°C fan/200°C/gas mark 6. Arrange the onions in a crowded single layer in a roasting dish, and tuck in the thyme. Drizzle over the oil and balsamic vinegar. Roast for 35–40 minutes until caramelised at the edges, stirring and seasoning the onions halfway through.

To make the risotto, bring the stock to the boil in a medium-size saucepan, season it with salt and keep it at a very gentle simmer throughout. Melt the butter in a large saucepan, add the onion and garlic, and cook them for a few minutes until they soften without allowing them to colour. Add the rice and cook it for about 1 minute, until it turns translucent and is coated with butter. Pour in the vermouth and once this has been absorbed start to add the stock a couple of ladles at a time – at no stage should the risotto be flooded. Stir it occasionally but not constantly.

Remove the pan from the heat while the risotto is a touch too moist and the rice still just firm and it should then arrive on the table the correct consistency. Stir in the lemon zest and juice, then the Parmesan and cream. Finally add the Emmental, three-quarters of the parsley and a generous grinding of black pepper. Taste to check for seasoning and serve straight away, scattered with the roasted onions and the rest of the parsley.

An oven-baked risotto may seem like heresy to staunch traditionalists, but having cooked it this way, you are unlikely to ever want to cook it any other. There is no being tied to the stove, just a little preparation at the beginning and again at the end, and plenty of time to relax in between.

oven-baked asparagus and vodka risotto

600g finger-thick asparagus
1.2 litres chicken stock (see page 31)
   or vegetable stock
50g unsalted butter
1 onion, peeled and finely chopped
300g risotto rice, e.g. Carnaroli
sea salt, black pepper
100g freshly grated Parmesan, plus
   extra shavings to serve
100ml lemon vodka
2 tablespoons lemon juice

Serves 4

Preheat the oven to 170°C fan/190°C/gas mark 5. Trim the asparagus spears where they become clearly fibrous and inedible (you can reserve the trimmings for stock). Peel the stalk to the point where it becomes green and tender, and cut the spears on the diagonal into 5cm lengths.

Bring the stock to the boil in a small saucepan. Melt half the butter in a large casserole over a medium heat, add the onion and cook for several minutes until softened, without colouring. Add the rice and stir for about 1 minute, then pour in the boiling stock, add some seasoning, cover and cook in the oven for 25 minutes.

In the meantime, bring a large pan of salted water to the boil. Add the asparagus spears and cook for about 5 minutes or until just tender, then drain them into a colander.

Add the remaining butter and the Parmesan to the rice and stir until it appears creamy and amalgamated. Stir in the vodka and lemon juice, and the asparagus, and briefly rewarm. Serve with extra Parmesan scattered over.

Another delightfully easy oven-cooked risotto, where the pesto is stirred into the rice as it comes out of the oven, giving it a vibrant boost as a final turn. Any young creamy goat's cheese will do for dolloping on top.

oven-baked risotto with pesto and goat's cheese

Risotto

1.2 litres chicken stock (see page 31) or vegetable stock
50g unsalted butter
1 onion, peeled and finely chopped
300g risotto rice, e.g. Carnaroli
150ml white wine
sea salt, black pepper
100g freshly grated Parmesan
100g fresh goat's cheese to serve

Pesto

1 shallot, peeled and chopped
30g pine nuts
80ml extra virgin olive oil
70g fresh basil leaves
a squeeze of lemon juice

Serves 4

Preheat the oven to 170°C fan/190°C/gas mark 5. Bring the stock to the boil in a small saucepan. Melt half the butter in a large casserole over a medium heat, add the onion and cook for several minutes until softened, without colouring. Add the rice and stir for about 1 minute, then pour in the wine and simmer until almost completely absorbed. Pour in the boiling stock, add some seasoning, cover and cook in the oven for 25 minutes.

In the meantime make the pesto. Place the shallot, pine nuts, olive oil and half the basil in a food processor with a little seasoning and whiz to a purée. Add the remaining basil and a squeeze of lemon juice and whiz briefly again. Taste for seasoning.

Add the remaining butter and the Parmesan to the rice and stir until it appears creamy and amalgamated. Spoon the pesto over, and loosely fold it in so that it streaks the rice. Serve with a dollop of goat's cheese on top.

fish

Fish for supper has always been a treat, and becomes ever more so as it grows increasingly scarce. When it comes to buying, the best advice I can give is to place your trust in a good local fishmonger, as this is an area fraught with complication even for those determined to shop ethically. And there is every chance that today's no-nos may be the fish-farming success stories of tomorrow.

That said, the best recipes for white fish keep an open mind as to which types can be used. Fish pies are ever adaptable, as are fishcakes, and a personal favourite is white fish and garlic butter roast.

I have never been against farmed salmon; wild salmon was already scarce by the time I began my cooking career, so spoilt hand-reared specimens have always been the norm. I don't even dislike their inherent oiliness. But like chicken, the difference between good and bad is considerable, and it is worth buying carefully. Do try the grilled salmon with pickled vegetables; it's a variation on the theme of *escabeche*, where aromatic juices infuse the fish as it cools, and it's yummy.

One cannot ignore the expense of good fish either, but there are still plenty of options that don't break the bank. I have lost count of the times I have picked up a bag of mussels from the fish counter without any particular plans for supper. The mussel stew is a lovely way of cooking them, with a thick, red and mushy sauce to be lapped up by some toast. Squid stews too are always a hit in this house, and now that it is so readily available fully prepared they couldn't be easier. Sometimes, though, it's the chips and tartare sauce that I'm after, and thankfully there are endless options for including those.

This is by way of sardines on toast, as much of a treat for supper as baked beans with a crispy fried egg on top. But there are tins and there are tins, so do seek out an old Breton name such as Connétable, aristos among tinned-fish producers. Either serve this with toast and a few salad leaves, or use it for toasted sarnies, and there's no shame in dishing it up as a starter or spreading it on little croûtons to hand round with drinks.

sardine pâté with celery salad

Pâté

3 x 100g tins of sardine fillets, drained
50g unsalted butter, softened
2 tablespoons finely chopped fresh flat-leaf parsley
1 small shallot, peeled and finely chopped
5 tablespoons extra virgin olive oil
2 tablespoons lemon juice
several shakes of Tabasco
sea salt
a few slivers of spring onion

Salad

1 celery heart, trimmed and thinly sliced diagonally
1 bunch of breakfast radishes (125g trimmed weight), thinly sliced lengthwise
125g black olives, pitted
a few fresh basil leaves, torn into strips
thin brown toast

Serves 4

Mash the sardines in a bowl, using a fork. In another bowl, work the butter until it's really soft and creamy, then add to the sardines with the parsley and shallot and blend. Work in a tablespoon each of olive oil and lemon juice, and season with a few shakes of Tabasco and a little salt. Pile into a pot and smooth the surface, then cover and chill until required. Shortly before serving, scatter some slivers of spring onion over.

To make the salad, combine the celery, radishes and olives. Dress with 4 tablespoons of olive oil, 1 tablespoon of lemon juice and a little salt, and toss in the basil. Serve the pâté and salad with thin brown toast.

Despite the fancy name these are basically homemade fish fingers, so out with the ketchup and petits pois if that's the order of the day. While lemon sole does very nicely, Dover sole makes for a deluxe version.

goujons of sole with tartare sauce

Goujons

200g fresh white or brown
  breadcrumbs
3 lemon sole fillets (approx.
  500g in total), skin on
sea salt, black pepper
4 tablespoons extra virgin olive
  oil
2 eggs, beaten
plain flour for dipping
lemon wedges to serve

Sauce

1 teaspoon grainy mustard
1 heaped tablespoon finely
  chopped gherkins
1 heaped tablespoon finely
  chopped capers
1 heaped tablespoon finely
  chopped fresh flat-leaf
  parsley
350g mayonnaise

Serves 6

Preheat the oven to 200°C fan/220°C/gas mark 7. Lay the breadcrumbs out in a thin layer on a baking tray and toast them for 6–8 minutes, until lightly golden. Remove and leave them to cool. Cut the fish fillets in half down the centre, and then in half again into fingers about 10cm long and 3–5cm wide. You may need to halve the widest fingers again. To make the tartare sauce, stir all the ingredients together in a bowl.

Scrunch the breadcrumbs between your fingers in a shallow bowl to break up any clumps and toss them with some seasoning and the olive oil until lightly coated. Place the eggs and flour in another couple of shallow bowls. Dip the fish first in the flour, then into the egg and breadcrumbs, and lay them out on a baking sheet or a roasting dish (you may need to use two). Bake them for 7–8 minutes, until lightly golden and crisp. Serve the goujons with the tartare sauce, and lemon wedges.

It's not often that scampi and chips can be regarded as healthy, but this is virtuous in its line-up of ingredients, and deliciously different from the usual offering. Here the scampi are coated in brown breadcrumbs and baked rather than fried, dished up with chips baked in the oven with lots of lemon and butter. They have that elusive, slightly leathery appeal of the roast potatoes your mum used to cook, and are crisp at the edges.

scampi 'n' chips

Scampi

200g fresh brown breadcrumbs
350g raw shelled king or tiger
    prawns
2 eggs, beaten
plain flour for dipping
coarsely chopped fresh parsley
    and lemon halves to serve

Chips

1.2kg large waxy potatoes, peeled
finely grated zest of 1 lemon,
    plus 1 tablespoon lemon juice
extra virgin olive oil
40g unsalted butter
sea salt, black pepper

Serves 4

Preheat the oven to 200°C fan/220°C/gas mark 7. Lay the breadcrumbs out in a thin layer on two baking trays and toast them for 6–8 minutes, until lightly golden. Remove and leave them to cool.

Slice the potatoes lengthwise 1cm thick, then cut them into thick chips. Arrange these in a roasting dish (about 38 x 25cm) with the lemon zest. Drizzle over 2 tablespoons of olive oil and the lemon juice, dot with the butter and season. Cover with foil and roast for 20 minutes. Loosen the chips with a spatula, give them a stir, and roast uncovered for another 30–35 minutes until deliciously golden and caramelised, stirring halfway through.

Towards the end of cooking the chips, dry the prawns on kitchen paper. Scrunch the breadcrumbs between your fingers to break up any clumps, and toss them in a shallow bowl with some seasoning and 4 tablespoons of oil until evenly and lightly coated. Have the eggs and flour at the ready in another couple of shallow bowls.

Coat the prawns a few at a time with the flour. Dip into the egg and then into the breadcrumbs and arrange on a large roasting tray, spaced slightly apart. Bake the scampi for 6–7 minutes, until crisp and lightly golden. Serve the scampi and chips straight away, scattered with parsley, accompanied by lemon halves.

As deliciously salty as you would expect any smoked haddock dish to be, I would serve these fishcakes with some pert little tomatoes roasted on the vine as a match. To this end, drizzle 400–500g of small tomatoes on the vine with a little vegetable oil and balsamic vinegar, season and roast in the oven for 15 minutes.

smoked haddock and almond fishcakes

600g maincrop potatoes, peeled
  and cut up if large
500g undyed smoked haddock fillet
100ml white wine
30g unsalted butter
sea salt, black pepper
2 tablespoons capers, rinsed
  and chopped
3 medium eggs
125g flaked almonds
50g fresh brown or white
  breadcrumbs
groundnut oil

Serves 4–6

Bring a medium-size pan of salted water to the boil. Add the potatoes and simmer for 20–30 minutes, until tender. At the same time, place the smoked haddock fillet skin down on the base of a medium-size pan, cutting it to fit in a single layer. Pour over the wine, dot with the butter and season with pepper. Bring to the boil, then cover the pan and cook over a low heat for 7 minutes. Using a spatula, transfer the fish to a plate and leave it to rest for 10 minutes.

Drain the potatoes into a sieve. Leave to steam dry for a few minutes, then mash them. Pour any juices given out by the fish back into the fish saucepan and reduce to a few tablespoons. Flake the haddock, discarding the skin, and mix it with the mashed potatoes and reduced emulsion. Stir in the capers and taste for seasoning. Now beat one of the eggs and blend into the mixture.

Using your hands, take a heaped tablespoon of the mixture at a time and shape into 12 fishcakes. Set them aside on a plate or a tray. They can be prepared to this point in advance, in which case cover and chill them.

Heat the oven to 200°C fan/220°C/gas mark 7. Place the flaked almonds in the bowl of a food processor and whiz to coarsely chop them, then combine them with the breadcrumbs in a shallow bowl. Whisk the remaining 2 eggs in another shallow bowl. Dip the fishcakes first in the beaten egg to coat them all over, then in the almond and breadcrumb mixture, and arrange them in one or two roasting dishes with a little oil drizzled over the base, spaced slightly apart. Drizzle over a little more oil and bake them for 30 minutes, turning them halfway through.

A big, fluffy, no-nonsense fishcake – that is my staple among this genre. Any white fish will do; the secret is the anchovy essence and the capers. Though a word on the essence, which can prove elusive – a little finely chopped anchovy can be used in its stead.

big fishcakes with parsley sauce

Fishcakes

600g maincrop potatoes, peeled
and halved or quartered if large
500g skinless white fish fillets
(cod, haddock, hake, etc.)
100ml white wine
30g unsalted butter
sea salt, black pepper
2 teaspoons anchovy essence
2 tablespoons capers, rinsed
and chopped
2 medium eggs
75g fresh brown or white
breadcrumbs
groundnut oil for shallow frying

Sauce

300g crème fraîche
1 heaped teaspoon Dijon mustard
5 tablespoons finely chopped
fresh parsley

Serves 6

Bring a medium-size pan of salted water to the boil. Add the potatoes and simmer for 20–25 minutes, until tender. At the same time, arrange the fish fillets in a single layer on the base of another medium-size saucepan. Pour over the wine, dot with the butter and season them. Bring the wine to the boil, then cover the pan and cook over a low heat for 7 minutes. Using a spatula, transfer the fish to a plate and leave it to rest for 10 minutes.

Drain the potatoes, leave for a few minutes to steam dry, then mash them. Pour any juices on the fish plate back into the saucepan and reduce to a few tablespoons, then stir in the anchovy essence. Flake the fish, discarding any bones, and mix it with the mashed potatoes. Pour over the cooking liquid, mix in the capers and season to taste.

Using your hands, shape the mixture into 6 large fishcakes. Beat the eggs in a shallow bowl, and place the breadcrumbs in another. Dip the fishcakes first in the beaten egg to coat them all over, and then in the breadcrumbs. Set aside on a plate.

To make the sauce, place the crème fraîche and mustard in a small saucepan and bring to the boil, giving it a whisk to blend in the mustard. Simmer for several minutes until you have a thin creamy sauce, then stir in the parsley and season with a pinch of salt. Transfer it to a bowl.

To cook the fishcakes, heat about 1cm of groundnut oil in a large frying pan over a medium heat, and cook the fishcakes in two batches for 2 minutes each side, or until golden and crisp. If necessary reheat the parsley sauce, without allowing it to boil, and serve with the fishcakes.

It's always a tough choice between the green chicken and the red prawn curry in a Thai restaurant. But I hold the latter especially dear ever since eating it for Christmas dinner on Ko Samui in Thailand, even if it has become an almost impossible battle to recreate the magic. As ever, rice is essential here for all those sweet and hot soupy juices (see page 111), and some prawn crackers would be rather nice too.

thai red prawn curry

Curry
5 tablespoons groundnut or vegetable oil
1½ heaped tablespoons red curry paste
2 red onions, peeled, halved and sliced
600ml coconut milk
2 tablespoons lime juice
1 tablespoon palm or light
    muscovado sugar

1½ teaspoons sea salt
700g raw peeled tiger prawns
a large handful of fresh basil leaves, torn
a large handful of fresh coriander leaves

Garnish (optional)
9 garlic cloves, peeled and sliced
3 medium-hot fresh red chillies, seeds
    removed and sliced

Serves 6

Heat 3 tablespoons of the oil in a large saucepan over a medium-low heat. Add the curry paste and stir it around, then add the onions and cook for a few minutes until they soften and are coated with the paste. Pour in the coconut milk and add the lime juice, sugar and salt. Bring to the boil and simmer over a very low heat for 15 minutes, stirring frequently, until the sauce is thick and creamy. Add the prawns, bring back to a simmer and cook for another 3–4 minutes, stirring occasionally, until tender and firm. Stir in the basil and coriander leaves. Taste to check the seasoning, adding a little more sugar or salt if necessary.

If serving the garnish, while the curry is cooking heat the remaining oil in a small frying pan over a medium heat and fry the garlic and chillies until the garlic is lightly coloured. Drain on kitchen paper and serve scattered over the curry.

A big roasting pan with shell-on prawns placed centrally to dip into couldn't make for a more convivial supper. But we're talking prize morsels here, so some cheese and a salad to follow, or brownies and ice cream, are essential to avoid midnight hunger pangs. You can spin it out though – the shells cast their bisque-like magic into the oil, and there's little problem in finding good use for a loaf of bread.

prawns in a pan

24 raw tiger prawns, shell on
6 tablespoons extra virgin olive oil
2 lemon quarters
4 tablespoons coarsely chopped fresh
    flat-leaf parsley
baguette or crusty white bread to serve

Serves 4

Preheat the oven to 220°C fan/240°C/gas mark 9. Place the prawns in a colander and give them a rinse under the cold tap, then shake them dry and arrange them in a single layer in one or two roasting dishes. Drizzle over the oil and roast for 10 minutes, then squeeze over the lemon and scatter over the parsley. Place the dishes centrally for everyone to help themselves, with plenty of bread for mopping up the juices in the pan.

Our love of milky white fish fillets is heavily ingrained and continues unabated, while the list of what we can eat with a clear conscience seems to ever diminish, and also changes. The good news is that more and more species are now being successfully farmed, and this will undoubtedly continue in the future.

So this recipe is not a recommendation of what you should be eating, rather one of how to cook whatever you have bought. It can be successfully applied to any white fish. Fillets are layered with a pungent garlic butter and smothered in breadcrumbs, so you end up with a thick hunk of butter-basted fish and a crisp coating on top. Some mash and a green salad or spinach would be just perfect.

white fish and garlic butter roast

Garlic Butter

125g unsalted butter, softened
4 garlic cloves, peeled and
   coarsely chopped
finely grated zest and juice of 1 lemon
a dash of Tabasco
sea salt, black pepper
3 tablespoons finely chopped
   fresh dill or fennel fronds
3 tablespoons finely chopped chives

Fish

1.2kg skinless whole haddock fillets
70g fresh white breadcrumbs
2 tablespoons extra virgin olive oil

Serves 6

Place the butter, garlic, lemon zest and juice, Tabasco and some seasoning in the bowl of a food processor and blend at high speed until creamy and amalgamated. Add the chopped herbs and give another quick whiz to incorporate them. Don't worry if a little of the lemon juice seeps out, most of it will have been incorporated.

Preheat the oven to 190°C fan/210°C/gas mark 6. Lightly season the upper side of each fish fillet, smear with the butter and arrange buttered side up in an 18 x 30cm/1.5 litre oval gratin or other shallow ovenproof dish, layering and cutting them to fit. Toss the breadcrumbs with the olive oil and scatter over. The fish can be prepared several hours in advance, in which case cover and chill the dish. Otherwise roast for 40 minutes until the crumbs are golden and crisp and the fish is cooked through – it should flake easily in the centre and have lost its translucency. Pour or spoon off the butter and juices at the sides, and serve these separately in a bowl or small jug for those that want them.

The haddock in this pie provides succulent flakes that hold their shape, but don't be constrained, buy whatever looks good that's within your budget.

normandy fish pie

Fish

800g haddock fillets, skin on
250ml milk
1 bay leaf
sea salt, black pepper
250g scallops, with corals
60g unsalted butter
50g plain flour
150ml dry cider
150g crème fraîche
1 heaped teaspoon Dijon mustard
200g shelled raw prawns
1 tablespoon small capers, rinsed

Mash

1.5kg maincrop potatoes, peeled
   and halved if large
100g crème fraîche
50g unsalted butter
2 large egg yolks

Serves 6

Place the haddock fillets in a large saucepan. Pour over the milk, tuck in the bay leaf, season and bring to the boil. Cover with a lid, leaving a gap for the steam to escape, and cook on a low heat for 4 minutes. Strain the cooking liquor into a bowl, and once the fish is cool enough to handle, flake it as coarsely as possible, discarding the skin. If any additional liquid is given out at this point, throw it away. Pull off the white gristle at the side of the scallops, removing the surrounding girdle, cut off and reserve the coral, and slice each scallop into 2 or 3 discs.

To make the béchamel, melt the butter in a medium-size non-stick saucepan, add the flour and allow to seethe for a minute. Very gradually work in the cider, the fish cooking liquor, then the crème fraîche and the mustard. Bring to the boil, stirring constantly, then simmer over a very low heat for 10 minutes, stirring occasionally. If any butter separates out, simply stir vigorously until it is reincorporated. Taste to check the seasoning, then fold in the haddock, scallops, prawns, reserved corals and capers. Transfer the fish to a 3.5 litre ovenproof dish; I use an oval gratin dish 25 x 35cm that affords a large crispy surface. Leave the fish to cool.

Bring a large pan of salted water to the boil. Add the potatoes and cook until tender. Drain and leave to steam dry for a minute or two. Pass through a mouli-légumes or a sieve back into the pan. Heat the crème fraîche with the butter and some seasoning and beat this into the mash, and then beat in the egg yolks. Smooth this over the top of the fish, forking the surface into furrows. You can cover and chill the pie until required, for up to 48 hours.

To cook the pie, preheat the oven to 180°C fan/200°C/gas mark 6 and bake it for 35–40 minutes, until crusty and golden on the surface.

Squid can only be Gemini — there are two routes to approaching them as different as the South Pole from the North. They need either to be seared very briefly on a hot grill, or slowly braised until meltingly tender. There is no in-between, and the first route is easier said than done at home without recourse to an industrially hot grill, so gentle stews are the better route. I would serve this spooned over a fluffy mound of rice (see page 111), a knob of salty butter in its midst.

squid and tomato stew

1kg squid (as long as your hand), fully
  prepared if possible

a pinch of saffron filaments
  (approx. 20)

5 tablespoons extra virgin olive oil,
  plus a little extra

1 Spanish onion, peeled, quartered
  and thinly sliced

4 garlic cloves, peeled and smashed
  with a rolling pin or the handle of
  a knife

2 beefsteak tomatoes, skinned
  and coarsely chopped

1 small dried chilli, finely chopped

sea salt

1 bay leaf

4 tablespoons brandy

125ml white wine

coarsely chopped fresh coriander
  to serve

Serves 4

If you're preparing the squid yourself, firmly the tug the head away from the body of each one to separate them. Remove the hard transparent pen from the body, and the thin membrane that covers it. Slit the pouch open and wash both sides, removing any remaining white membranes. Slice the open pouches and halve if the slices are long. Cut the tentacles from the head above the eyes, and halve if large.

Pour 1 tablespoon of boiling water over the saffron in a small bowl and leave to infuse. Heat 3 tablespoons of olive oil in a large frying pan over a medium heat, add the onion and garlic and cook over a low heat for about 5 minutes until soft but not coloured, stirring occasionally. Add the tomatoes, chilli and a little salt and sauté, mushing the tomatoes down with a wooden spoon until the juices given out evaporate.

Heat the remaining olive oil in a medium-size saucepan over a medium-high heat. Add the squid, salt and bay leaf, and stir regularly until the squid has thrown off its liquid and is seething. Add the brandy, flambéing it if you are brave. The easiest way to do this is to pour in all but a little of the brandy, warm this in a metal spoon over a flame and as soon as it ignites pour it into the pan and the rest will flare up. But this isn't essential.

Add the wine, bring to the boil and simmer for a few minutes to reduce it, then add the sautéd vegetables. Bring back to the boil and simmer uncovered over a low heat for about 50 minutes, stirring regularly until the squid is tender and coated in a thick sauce. Add the saffron liquid about 10 minutes before the end. Transfer to a bowl, drizzle over a little more oil and scatter with chopped coriander.

As simple as moules marinière with an Italian bent, lots of tomatoes and a hint of chilli. And like all the best mussel dishes it's as much soup as stew. Sucking the sauce off the shells and extracting the morsels within is the best bit, so I wouldn't worry overly about shelling them unless you're feeling particularly energetic.

mussel stew with tomato and chilli

1.5kg mussels
150ml white wine
3 garlic cloves, peeled
extra virgin olive oil
4 tablespoons chopped fresh
    flat-leaf parsley
1 x 400g tin of chopped tomatoes
1 small dried chilli, finely chopped
4 x 1cm slices of baguette

Serves 4

Wash the mussels in a sink of cold water, discarding any that are damaged or do not close when tapped sharply against the surface. Pull off any beards, then wash the mussels a second time. Place them in a large saucepan with the wine, cover, and cook over a high heat for 5 minutes, by which time they should have opened. Remove them to a bowl and decant the cooking liquor, discarding the gritty bit at the bottom. If you like you can shell half the mussels.

Finely chop 2 of the garlic cloves. Heat 3 tablespoons of olive oil in a large saucepan over a medium heat, add the chopped garlic and half the parsley and sizzle for 30 seconds until the garlic just begins to colour. Add the tomatoes and chilli. Turn the heat down and cook very gently for about 15 minutes, stirring occasionally, until the oil rises to the surface and separates out from the tomatoes.

The stew can be prepared to this point a few hours in advance. To serve it, add the mussel juices to the tomato base and heat together, then add the mussels to the pan, cover, and reheat for a couple of minutes, stirring once. Toast the bread, give the croûtons a rub with the reserved garlic clove and place in the base of four soup bowls. Splash over a little olive oil, ladle the stew on top, then scatter over the remaining parsley and splash some more olive oil over.

This is a great way of cooking salmon fillets, turning the skin into a gorgeously crisp sheathe, while the flesh remains beautifully succulent.

crispy salmon with mustard cream

Salmon

1 tablespoon extra virgin olive or
 groundnut oil
finely grated zest of 1 lemon
6 x 150g salmon fillets, skin on

Sauce

150g crème fraîche
1½ teaspoons grainy mustard
2 teaspoons finely chopped fresh
 tarragon

Cabbage

50g unsalted butter
150g unsmoked rindless streaky bacon,
 diced
1 small white cabbage, outer leaves
 discarded, quartered, core removed,
 finely sliced
1 small Savoy cabbage, outer leaves
 discarded, quartered, core removed,
 finely sliced
sea salt, black pepper

Serves 6

Preheat the oven to 180°C fan/200°C/gas mark 6. Combine the oil and lemon zest in a small bowl and rub all over the salmon fillets on a plate. Set aside for 15 minutes. Blend all the ingredients for the sauce together in a bowl and set aside.

Heat half the butter in a large saucepan over a medium-high heat, add the bacon and fry for 5–6 minutes until it starts to colour, stirring frequently. Add half the cabbage and cook for about 4 minutes until wilted but still crisp, seasoning it with black pepper halfway through. Transfer this to a bowl and cook the remaining cabbage in the same way. Put all the cabbage back into the pan.

At the same time as cooking the cabbage, heat a large non-stick frying pan over a medium-high heat and season the salmon fillets on both sides. You will probably need to cook them in two batches. First colour the skin for 4–5 minutes, then turn and sear the flesh for 30 seconds and transfer them to a roasting dish skin side up, spaced a little way apart. Roast for 6–8 minutes – you can slip a knife through the centre of the thickest fillet to see if it is done. It should be faintly translucent, just cooked.

Reheat the cabbage if necessary, then serve with the salmon and the sauce spooned over.

I can't get enough of all-in-ones: here, salmon with a little vegetable salad in a dressing that sings with saffron. And it can be made several hours or even a day in advance of eating. You could also serve it with a tomato salad, and some warm new potatoes or bread.

grilled salmon with pickled vegetables

Salmon

extra virgin olive oil
sea salt, black pepper
6 x 150g salmon fillets, skin on

Pickle

150ml dry white wine
1½ tablespoons white wine vinegar
2 slim carrots, trimmed, peeled and
   thinly sliced
1 leek, trimmed and thinly sliced
130g small (1–2cm) cauliflower florets
2 bay leaves
3 garlic cloves, peeled and smashed
a pinch of saffron filaments
   (approx. 20)
a pinch of chilli flakes
½ teaspoon caster sugar

Serves 6

Place 2 tablespoons of olive oil, 150ml of water and 1 teaspoon of salt in a small saucepan with the pickle ingredients. Bring to the boil and simmer for about 20 minutes (making sure they're submerged), until the vegetables are tender.

Meanwhile, heat a large non-stick frying pan over a medium heat. Brush the salmon fillets with olive oil and season on both sides. You will need to cook the fillets in batches. Fry for 4–6 minutes skin side down until golden and you can see from the sides that the fish is cooked at least halfway through. Turn and fry the flesh side for 1–2 minutes, leaving the fish slightly underdone in the centre; it should still give a little if you press it.

Arrange the fish skin side up in a shallow dish that holds the fillets fairly snugly, but with a little space in between. Stir 2 tablespoons of oil into the hot pickle and pour it over the fish, which should be covered by about two-thirds. Loosely cover and leave to cool completely for about 3 hours. This can be made up to a day in advance, in which case chill and bring back to room temperature an hour before eating.

This is something like the old-fashioned risottos of my childhood, which were basically rice dishes filled with treasures, and you could raid the storecupboard for zesty little sauces as it suited you. On this note a jar of mayo might go down even better than the Parmesan, but don't be constrained, let your imagination wander.

oven-baked saffron rice with prawns and scallops

1 litre fish stock
75g unsalted butter
1 onion, peeled and finely chopped
325g risotto rice, e.g. Carnaroli
150ml white wine
a pinch of saffron filaments (approx. 20),
    ground and blended with 1
    tablespoon boiling water
sea salt, black pepper
6 scallops, with corals
300g raw shelled tiger prawns
50g grated Parmesan

Serves 4–6

Preheat the oven to 200°C fan/220°C/gas mark 7. Bring the stock to the boil in a small saucepan. Melt 50g of the butter in a medium-size saucepan over a medium heat, and sauté the onion for several minutes until softened. Add the rice and stir for about a minute until glossy, then pour in the wine and simmer until absorbed. Add the stock, the saffron liquor and some seasoning and bring to the boil. Tip the mixture into a 35cm/2.5 litre gratin dish or other shallow ovenproof dish, evenly distributing the rice over the base. Cover with foil and bake for 15 minutes.

To prepare the scallops, remove the girdle around the scallop and with it the coral. Reserving the coral, cut off and discard the small white gristle, and slit the scallops in half.

Season the seafood and stir into the rice, scatter the Parmesan over and dot with the remaining butter. Return it to the oven, uncovered, for another 15 minutes, until the rice is tender – it should be loose and creamy. Like a rice pudding, it will be wetter on the surface than underneath. Serve straight away.

birds

Sometimes I set out to prove to my husband that there is a point when you can get bored with eating chicken. But even after a week of it, night after night, he is happy to face it again the following day, so I have more or less conceded defeat on this one. The good news is its sheer adaptability – it lends itself to more ways of being served than any other meat I can think of.

Of various small cuts, I have a particular soft spot for wings that are all skin and very little flesh, so you end up with gorgeously crisp and sticky finger food when they're roasted in the oven or grilled on a barbecue. Thighs and drumsticks are great for casseroles and curries, providing not only a tasty stock but also succulent slivers of dark meat, where a breast would simply dry out. But there are times when a thin chicken escalope dipped into breadcrumbs and fried, served with a dollop of mayonnaise or garlic butter, provides just the right kind of glamour with a crisp green salad. And the advantage here is that one breast will do for two.

If I am going to cook a whole chook mid-week, I invariably pot-roast it. This is a great way of cooking a bird: first you sear and colour the skin, then you pop it into a casserole with a tightly fitting lid with a glass of wine or stock and a few aromatics, and it effectively steams, emerging beautifully succulent and moist with a pool of juices for the gravy or the basis of a creamy sauce. It's a very friendly method that you can play around with endlessly to suit whatever you have to hand.

But there is one caveat to this suppertime great, and that is the gap between good and bad, which makes for completely different products. Buy the very best, a promise of breed and good husbandry that will in turn deliver a toothsome texture and flavour. The starting point is free-range. If you are buying from a small producer then even better.

A little pâté is every bit as welcome after a bowl of soup as a slice of cheese, and this will keep well for at least 48 hours, so you can eke it out in all manner of ways. Served with a thick slab of toast, a dollop of chutney, breakfast radishes, some gherkins and pickled onions, it is just the ticket if you've been out early evening and want something almost instant afterwards. This one is velvety as butter – I normally make it in a bowl and spoon it out.

farmhouse chicken liver pâté

225g unsalted butter
225g chicken livers*, fatty
  membranes removed
1 bay leaf
2 sprigs of fresh thyme
sea salt, black pepper
1 shallot, peeled and finely chopped
1 garlic clove, peeled and
  finely chopped
2 tablespoons Calvados or brandy
1 tablespoon crème fraîche
freshly grated nutmeg
chutney, cocktail gherkins, pickled
  onions, radishes, watercress,
  toasted walnut bread to serve

Serves 4

Melt 25g of the butter in a large frying pan over a medium heat. Add the chicken livers and the herbs. Season, and sauté for 3 minutes until they are golden on the outside but still pink in the centre, turning the livers halfway through. Discard the herbs and tip the livers with any juices into a blender.

Add another knob of butter to the pan and sweat the shallot and garlic for a couple of minutes until glossy and translucent. Add the Calvados and simmer until it has all but disappeared. Tip into the blender and purée with the crème fraîche. Leave this to cool for about 20 minutes, then dice the remaining butter, add to the blender and purée until the pâté is really smooth and creamy. Add a grinding of nutmeg and adjust the seasoning. Pass the pâté through a fine sieve to ensure it's as silky as possible, if you like. Spoon it into a bowl, smooth the surface, cover and chill until required. Leave it for 20 minutes out of the fridge for it to soften before serving.

Serve the paté by the spoonful, accompanied by chutney, gherkins, pickled onions, radishes, watercress and toasted walnut bread.

* It's unusual to find fresh chicken livers, so look in the freezer section.

Most children will swim an ocean for a plate of sticky crispy chicken wings to nibble at; combine them with a tikka marinade and they should be in heaven. You might even get a crisp little salad of young lettuce leaves, finely sliced radishes, avocado and spring onion down them at the same time. I'd throw some warm puffy flatbread into the equation too.

chicken tikka wings

12 free-range chicken wings

a few limes, quartered

a few whole medium-hot fresh red
   chillies

Marinade

3 tablespoons plain yoghurt

2 tablespoons groundnut
   or vegetable oil

1 teaspoon turmeric

1 teaspoon ground cumin

5 cardamom pods, inside seeds ground

⅛ teaspoon ground cloves
   (i.e. about 2 cloves)

½ teaspoon cayenne pepper

a squeeze of lemon juice

2 cloves of garlic, peeled and puréed

2 teaspoons coarsely grated
   fresh ginger

1 heaped teaspoon sea salt

Serves 4–6

Combine all the ingredients for the marinade in a large bowl or container. Add the chicken wings and coat, then cover and marinate for 30 minutes. Preheat the oven to 200°C fan/220°C/gas mark 7, and arrange the chicken wings skin side down in a couple of roasting dishes, spaced slightly apart. Tuck in the quarters of lime and the chillies and roast for 30 minutes, turning the wings back up the right way halfway through. The lower tray may take a few minutes longer. Those who like extra seasoning can squeeze a little of the lime pulp over the chicken wings, with the inside of the chillies.

A thin juicy escalope coated in crisp golden breadcrumbs with a squeeze of lemon and a smattering of parsley has to be one of the best ways of serving chicken breasts – strains of the Italian Riviera. Bettered only perhaps by a dollop of garlic butter melting over the top in reference to chicken Kiev.

chicken escalopes

2 skinless free-range chicken breasts
sea salt, black pepper
100g fresh white breadcrumbs
extra virgin olive oil
lemon wedges and coarsely chopped
   fresh flat-leaf parsley to serve

Serves 4

Halve the chicken breasts into thin escalopes, cutting out the white membrane on the underside if it is evident. Season the breadcrumbs in a bowl, and dip the escalopes first in extra virgin olive oil, and then in the breadcrumbs, pressing them in. Set aside for 10 minutes.

Heat a couple of tablespoons of olive oil in a large frying pan over a medium heat and fry the escalopes in batches for a few minutes each side until golden. Serve hot or cold with lemon wedges and chopped flat-leaf parsley, or as opposite.

The essence of chicken Kiev is the melted butter than spills from within the breast when you cut into it. But I can never be bothered with all that dipping and deep-frying. This butter is simply the inside of chicken Kiev without the hassle. Serve with a salad of lamb's lettuce or watercress.

near instant kiev garlic butter

100g unsalted butter, softened
3 garlic cloves, peeled and
  coarsely chopped
zest and juice of 1 lemon
a dash of Tabasco
sea salt, black pepper
3 tablespoons finely chopped fresh
  flat-leaf parsley
2 tablespoons finely chopped fresh
  chives
1 teaspoon finely chopped fresh
  thyme leaves

Place the butter, garlic, lemon zest and juice, Tabasco and some seasoning in the bowl of a food processor and blend at high speed until creamy and amalgamated. Add the chopped herbs and give another quick whiz to incorporate them. Don't worry if a little of the lemon juice seeps out, most of it will have been incorporated. Place the butter on a strip of cling film and wrap it up, forming a smooth cylinder, twisting both ends. Chill for at least 30 minutes.

Preheat the grill. Place the cooked chicken escalopes on plates, with a couple of slices of the garlic butter on top. Even though this may appear to be a lot of butter, it is mainly herbs. Flash under the grill until it melts and serve straight away.

Just the mention of preserved lemons and olives in a chicken tagine sets the mouth watering. This is a slightly unusual take on this classic, in that the chicken is first marinated and poached, then roasted at the end in a hot oven to colour it, so you get the best of both worlds. Warm flatbreads or a fluffy mound of couscous are the order of the day here.

chicken tagine with preserved lemons and olives

1 preserved lemon, rinsed
2 garlic cloves, peeled and
  coarsely chopped
2cm piece of fresh ginger, peeled
  and coarsely chopped
¼ teaspoon ground ginger
¼ teaspoon turmeric
4 tablespoons extra virgin olive oil
8 free-range chicken thighs
1 large onion, peeled and cut up
a pinch of saffron filaments (approx.
  20), ground and blended with 1
  tablespoon boiling water
sea salt, black pepper
75g green olives, pitted
1 tablespoon lemon juice
chopped fresh coriander to serve

Serves 4

Quarter the preserved lemon, remove the pulp from the skin and purée this in a food processor with the garlic, fresh ginger, ground ginger, turmeric and 2 tablespoons of the oil. Coat the chicken thighs with this paste, cover and chill, ideally overnight but at least for a couple of hours. Reserve some lemon skin.

Preheat the oven to 200°C fan/220°C/gas mark 7. Place the onion in a food processor and reduce to a pulp (you could also grate it by hand, but only at the risk of a stream of tears). Put the chicken into a cast-iron casserole with the grated onion, the saffron, and some salt and pepper. Pour over 150ml of water, and give everything a good stir. Bring to a simmer, then cover and braise over a low heat for 15 minutes.

Transfer the chicken pieces to a baking tray, skin side up. Drizzle over the remaining 2 tablespoons of oil and place the tray in the oven for 20 minutes until the chicken is lightly golden. At the same time, skim any excess fat off the juices in the casserole. Add the olives and the lemon juice and simmer the sauce for a few minutes to reduce and thicken it. Taste to check the seasoning. Serve the chicken in warm shallow bowls with the sauce spooned over, scattered with coriander and a piece or two of lemon skin.

I love the nutty texture of this pilaf – the bulgar wheat soaks up all the flavours of the aromatics, while chicken, bacon and pistachios are star morsels, though you could also use cashews or toasted flaked almonds.

chicken and bulgar wheat with pistachios

1 tablespoon extra virgin olive oil
sea salt, black pepper
8 free-range chicken drumsticks
3 rashers of rindless unsmoked
  streaky bacon, diced
1 white onion, peeled, halved
  and sliced
225g bulgar wheat, rinsed
  in a sieve
150ml white wine
300ml chicken stock (see page
  31)
1 bay leaf
2 sprigs of fresh thyme
2 x 5cm strips of lemon zest
3 tablespoons coarsely chopped
  fresh flat-leaf parsley
40g roasted and salted
  pistachios, shelled and
  coarsely chopped
lemon wedges and tomato
  chutney to serve

Serves 4

Heat the olive oil in a large saucepan. Season the chicken drumsticks and cook them quite slowly for 15–20 minutes over a medium heat until they are coloured on all sides, then remove them from the pan. Add the bacon and cook until it begins to colour, then put it to one side with the chicken. Add the onion and cook for about 10 minutes over a medium heat, stirring occasionally until it is soft and lightly coloured.

Add the bulgar wheat and stir, then return the chicken and bacon to the pan. Pour in the wine and stock and season generously. Bring the liquid to the boil, add the herbs and lemon zest, cover with a tightly fitting lid and cook over a low heat for 10 minutes, by which time all the liquid should have been absorbed.

Without removing the lid, turn the heat off and leave it for 15 minutes, during which time it will dry out further and become more tender. Give the pilaf a stir to fluff up the bulgar wheat, and remove the herbs and lemon zest. Toss in the parsley and serve scattered with pistachios. Accompany with lemon wedges and tomato chutney.

This is a classic that we have all come to know and love. One of the best bits of an authentic Thai green chicken curry are those little pea aubergines that burst in the mouth; here I've added green peas to the same effect. I normally take the easy route with this curry and buy the best ready-made paste I can find rather than starting from scratch – there are some excellent ones around, and you may even have access to a Thai deli.

thai green chicken curry

6 free-range chicken breasts, skinned

4 tablespoons groundnut
 or vegetable oil

sea salt

8 shallots, peeled and sliced

2 garlic cloves, peeled and sliced

2 level tablespoons Thai green
 curry paste

425ml chicken stock (see page 31)

2 x 400ml tins of coconut milk

6 lime leaves

4 whole medium-hot fresh red chillies

200g shelled peas (fresh or frozen)

3 tablespoons fish sauce

1 rounded tablespoon caster sugar

20g fresh basil leaves

20g fresh coriander leaves

cooked rice (see opposite) and lime
 wedges to serve

Serves 6

Pull off the inner fillet on the underside of each chicken breast, and cut either side of the tendon to remove it, leaving two strips. Halve these if they seem long. Slice the remaining chicken breasts across into strips 1cm wide, again cutting out any white tendon, and halving any very thick slices into thin strips. Heat half the oil in a large frying pan over a high heat and colour the chicken in several batches, seasoning it with salt, removing it to a bowl as you go.

Heat the remaining oil in a large casserole or saucepan over a medium-low heat, and cook the shallots and garlic for a few minutes until they soften. Stir in the curry paste and cook for 1 minute longer, then add the stock, one of the tins of coconut milk, the lime leaves and the whole chillies. Bring to the boil over a high heat, then simmer over a low heat for 10 minutes. You can prepare the recipe to this point in advance and finish cooking it 10 minutes before you want to eat.

Bring the sauce back to the boil over a medium heat, add the chicken and peas and simmer for 5 minutes. Stir the remaining tin of coconut milk, the fish sauce, sugar and herbs into the curry, and bring back to the boil.

Serve the curry ladled over rice and accompany with lime wedges – you can leave in the whole chillies and lime leaves and remove them as you are eating.

fluffy rice

This method of cooking rice allows for a little leeway in timing, and it will stand around for longer than the allocated 20 minutes if you're not quite ready to eat.

For six people, measure out 400g of basmati or jasmine rice, soak it in a bowl of cold water for 30 minutes, then rinse it under the cold tap. If you're short on time, however, simply rinse it. Place it in a medium-size saucepan with a little under double the quantity of water (about 700ml) and a teaspoon of salt. Bring to the boil, skimming off any foam that rises to the surface initially, and simmer for 8–10 minutes. Clamp on a lid, turn off the heat and leave for 20 minutes, then fluff the rice up with a fork.

I have a particular soft spot for potato curries, especially when there is ginger and tomato in there too, so this chicken dopiaza is a winner on my list. The lively little relish is like a salad, and enlivens the curry. Some poppadums on the side would go down well too.

chicken and potato dopiaza

Dopiaza

1 teaspoon chilli powder

4 tablespoons groundnut oil

2 bay leaves

1 x 7cm cinnamon stick, broken in half

6 garlic cloves, peeled and finely chopped

6 cardamom pods

4 cloves

3 whole medium-hot fresh red chillies

2 teaspoons ginger purée, or finely grated fresh ginger

2 heaped tablespoons tomato purée

½ teaspoon turmeric

1 teaspoon caster sugar

1 free-range chicken, jointed into 8 pieces

8 small new potatoes, scrubbed or peeled

2 tomatoes, chopped

sea salt

2 onions, peeled and chopped

Relish

¼ green pepper, seeds and membranes removed, and finely diced

¼ red onion, peeled and finely diced

1 tomato, core removed and finely diced

a squeeze of lemon juice

Serves 4

Blend the chilli powder with 1 tablespoon of water to a paste in a small bowl. Heat half the oil in a large casserole over a medium heat, add the bay leaves, cinnamon and garlic, and once this starts to sizzle add the cardamom pods, cloves and red chillies. Stir and add the ginger, chilli paste, tomato purée, turmeric and sugar. Add the chicken, potatoes and tomatoes, stir to coat thoroughly, and cook for about 10 minutes, stirring frequently.

Now season with salt and add 300ml of water. Bring to a simmer, then cover and cook over a low heat for 1 hour. Heat the remaining oil in a large frying pan over a medium heat and fry the onions for about 10 minutes, stirring frequently, until they are golden. Set aside in a bowl.

Just before the chicken is cooked, combine all the ingredients for the relish with a pinch of salt in a bowl. Finally stir the fried onions into the curry and taste to check the seasoning. The whole spices and chillies can be picked out as you are eating. Accompany with the tomato and pepper relish.

A traybake is a great way of turning out a complete roast dinner in one – everything emerges golden and crisp, the reason we love a roast so much in the first place. A really simple, crisp green salad would be lovely with this.

chicken and new potato traybake

1kg small new potatoes, skin on

4 bay leaves

extra virgin olive oil

sea salt, black pepper

8 free-range chicken thighs,
    or chicken pieces

paprika

3 red onions, peeled, halved and sliced

1 head of garlic, broken into cloves

juice of ½ lemon

230ml mayonnaise

1 tablespoon finely chopped fresh
    tarragon

Serves 4

Preheat the oven to 190°C fan/210°C/gas mark 6. Bring a large pan of salted water to the boil. Add the potatoes and cook for 10 minutes, then drain them. Arrange them in a large roasting dish with the bay leaves, pour over 4 tablespoons of olive oil, season with salt and pepper and roast for 10 minutes.

In the meantime, heat a tablespoon of oil in a large frying pan over a medium-high heat. Season the chicken thighs with salt and paprika, and fry on both sides until really golden. If necessary do this in batches.

Stir the onions and garlic cloves into the potatoes, coating them with oil, then tuck in the chicken thighs, skin side up. Pour over the lemon juice and roast the traybake for another 50 minutes. At the same time, mix the mayonnaise and the chopped tarragon. Cover and chill until required.

Serve the chicken and vegetables with the tarragon mayonnaise. You can squeeze the garlic out of its skin and eat this too.

Yet another all-in-one, rare roast duck breasts with beetroot and onions that are rendered sweet and syrupy, cooked in duck fat and olive oil that is poured off at the end.

duck with beetroot and onion confit

700g raw beetroot, peeled and cut into thin wedges
extra virgin olive oil
sea salt, black pepper
4 red onions, peeled, halved and thinly sliced
6 thick slices of fresh ginger
¾ teaspoon five-spice powder
4 duck breasts, skin on
1 tablespoon balsamic vinegar
coarsely chopped fresh flat-leaf parsley to serve

Serves 4

Preheat the oven to 180°C fan/200°C/gas mark 6. Arrange the beetroot in a large roasting tray (about 38 x 25cm), pour over 2 tablespoons of olive oil, season and toss, and cook for 20 minutes.

Scatter the onions and ginger over the beetroot and drizzle over another couple of tablespoons of oil. Season and give the vegetables a stir, then roast for another 25 minutes.

At the same time, heat a large frying pan over a high heat. Rub the five-spice powder into the skin of the duck breasts. Season them and fry skin side down for several minutes, until golden, then drain off the fat, turn and briefly sear the flesh side to colour it. You will probably need to do them in two batches, removing them to a plate as you go.

Take the vegetables out of the oven, drizzle with the balsamic vinegar and give them a stir. Settle the duck breasts skin side up between them and put back into the oven for another 15 minutes. Remove the duck breasts to a board and leave to rest for 5 minutes. Discard the ginger, tip the roasting tray to collect the juices in the corner, and spoon off any excess fat, leaving the ruby beetroot juices behind. Slice the duck breasts, or provide everyone with steak knives. Serve with the vegetables, scattered with parsley.

This is half soup and half stew, replete with the two stars of cock-a-leekie, the leeks and the prunes. You'll want a big floury baked potato or a pan of buttery boiled spuds.

'cock-a-leekie' guinea fowl casserole

25g unsalted butter
1 tablespoon groundnut or
   vegetable oil
sea salt, black pepper
1 x 1.2kg guinea fowl, jointed
150ml white wine
700ml chicken stock (see
   page 31)

1 bay leaf
500g leeks (trimmed weight),
   thinly sliced
12 'no-need-to-soak'
   prunes, pitted
coarsely chopped fresh
   flat-leaf parsley to serve

Serves 4

Heat the butter and oil in a large cast-iron casserole over a medium heat. Season the guinea fowl pieces and colour on both sides, if necessary in two batches. Return all the pieces to the pan, and add the wine, stock, bay leaf and some seasoning. Bring to the boil, cover and simmer for 20 minutes.

Add the leeks and prunes, submerging them in the stock, then cover and cook for another 25 minutes. Serve the casserole with lots of parsley scattered over.

Any potato-topped pie does it in our house, like here, where coarsely crushed potatoes splashed with a little olive oil turn divinely crispy.

chicken and caper pie

extra virgin olive oil

sea salt, black pepper

12 free-range chicken thighs

3 garlic cloves, peeled and crushed to a paste

3 heaped tablespoons flour

150ml white wine

225ml chicken stock (see page 31) or water

4 sprigs of fresh thyme

a couple of strips of lemon zest

125g crème fraîche

2 tablespoons capers, rinsed

1.3kg medium or large waxy potatoes, e.g. Charlotte, peeled and halved or quartered as necessary

4 tablespoons coarsely chopped fresh flat-leaf parsley

Serves 6

Heat a tablespoon of olive oil in a large saucepan over a medium-high heat, season the chicken thighs and colour them on both sides, 6 at a time. Just before the end of cooking the second batch, drain off all but a tablespoon of the fat, then stir in the garlic and cook for a moment. Return all the chicken to the pan, sprinkle over the flour and turn the chicken to coat it. Add the wine, which will thicken as it blends with the flour, and let this seethe for a moment. Pour in the chicken stock or water and stir (don't worry about a few tiny lumps, as it's sieved at the end). Add the thyme, lemon zest and seasoning. Bring the sauce to a simmer, cover and cook over a low heat for 30 minutes, stirring once.

Remove the chicken pieces to a bowl. Once they are cool enough to handle, remove and discard the skin and coarsely shred the flesh. Skim any fat off the surface of the sauce and strain it through a sieve into a small non-stick pan. Simmer to reduce by about half, then stir in the crème fraîche and capers and adjust the seasoning. Stir into the chicken and transfer to a 20 x 30cm roasting or ovenproof dish.

Bring a large pan of salted water to the boil. Add the potatoes and simmer until tender, then drain them into a colander and leave for a few minutes for the surface moisture to evaporate. Now mash them very coarsely, partly chopping them with the side of the masher. Stir in 3 tablespoons of olive oil and some salt, and then the parsley. Spoon the potato on top of the chicken. The pie can be prepared in advance to this point, in which case leave it to cool, then cover and chill.

Preheat the oven to 180°C fan/200°C/gas mark 6 and bake the pie for 35–40 minutes, until golden and crisp at the tips.

A chicken fricassee is as luxurious as it is simple. For anyone with a soft spot for chicken and rice, it's yummy ladled over a fluffy mound of basmati (see page 111), or serve with some buttery new potatoes with a mint sprig in their midst.

chicken fricassée

Gently melt the butter in a small saucepan. Skim off the surface foam, decant the clarified butter and discard the milky solids below. Heat the clarified butter in a large cast-iron casserole over a medium heat. Season the chicken thighs on both sides and colour the flesh side for about 7 minutes until nicely golden, then turn and colour the skin side for about another 7 minutes, again until nicely golden. Tuck the tarragon sprigs between the chicken thighs, cover the pan and cook over a low heat for 30 minutes until the chicken is tender and comes away from the bone easily.

Halfway through the cooking time, bring a medium-size pan of salted water to the boil. Add the peas and mangetouts and cook for 2 minutes, then drain into a sieve. At the same time turn the chicken thighs.

Remove the chicken to a bowl and skim the chicken juices of fat if you like; otherwise in for a penny, the butter simply makes for a richer sauce. Add the wine to the pan juices and simmer for a few minutes to reduce by half. Add the crème fraîche and simmer for a minute or two longer until you have a creamy amalgamated sauce, then discard the tarragon and stir in the peas and mangetouts. Serve the chicken with the sauce spooned over, scattered with parsley if wished.

50g unsalted butter
sea salt, black pepper
8 free-range chicken thighs, skin on
4 sprigs of fresh tarragon
200g shelled fresh peas
150g mangetouts, topped and tailed
100ml white wine
200ml crème fraîche
1 tablespoon coarsely chopped fresh
    flat-leaf parsley to serve (optional)

Serves 4

A pot-roast is my stock way of cooking a whole chicken mid-week. The bird emerges beautifully succulent, in a plentiful pool of juices that serve as a gravy. You need a heavy cast-iron casserole here, with a tight-fitting lid, as the chicken cooks in the smallest amount of wine. If in any doubt, you can add up to another 150ml of chicken stock or water to the pot with the wine, thicken the juices at the end with a teaspoon of flour mashed with a teaspoon of butter, and simmer until nice and rich.

pot-roast chicken with wild rice

a pinch of saffron filaments (approx. 20)

1 x 1.6kg free-range chicken

groundnut or vegetable oil

sea salt, black pepper

4 x 5cm sprigs of fresh rosemary

150ml white wine

30g flaked almonds

250g wild and white rice mix, rinsed in a sieve

150g crème fraîche

6 spring onions, trimmed and cut into 2 or 3, then cut into fine strips

Serves 4–5

Preheat the oven to 180°C fan/200°C/gas mark 6. Pour a tablespoon of boiling water over the saffron and leave to infuse. Coat the chicken with oil and season it. Heat a frying pan over a high heat and colour the chicken on all sides, then place it breast up in a large cast-iron casserole. Add the rosemary and wine, bring to a simmer, then cover the casserole and cook in the oven for 55 minutes. Check it halfway through, and if it appears to be drying out add a little water or chicken stock. While the chicken is cooking, spread the almonds in a thin layer in a small ovenproof dish and toast for 8–10 minutes, until lightly coloured.

About 20 minutes before the end of cooking, bring a large pan of salted water to the boil for the rice, which will take about 20 minutes if you are using a mix. So add this to the water 5 minutes before the chicken is ready.

Uncover the chicken and leave it to rest in the pan for 15 minutes. Remove the chicken to a plate, pouring any juices inside back into the pan. Skim any excess fat off the juices in the pan and remove the rosemary. Add the saffron liquor and crème fraîche, bring back to the boil and simmer for a few minutes until you have a thin but rich sauce. Taste for seasoning.

Drain the rice and leave it to stand for a couple of minutes, then toss in the spring onions. Carve the chicken and serve on a bed of rice, with the sauce poured over, scattered with almonds.

Just to prove that anything chicken can do guinea fowl can do better, here's a favourite classic, replete with button mushrooms and baby onions. You'll need something for mopping up all the rich red juices, either some warm crusty bread or potatoes – baked, boiled or mashed as takes your fancy. The red wine needn't be anything special; cheap, cheerful and with plenty of character.

This is a casserole that reheats well, with the added advantage if you allow it to cool completely that you can scrape off any fat that has risen to the surface.

'coq au vin'

1 tablespoon groundnut or vegetable oil
1.2kg guinea fowl, jointed into 8
    pieces*
sea salt, black pepper
75g unsmoked rindless streaky bacon,
    sliced
1 heaped tablespoon flour
600ml red wine
150ml chicken stock (see page 31)
1 bay leaf
2 sprigs of fresh thyme
10g unsalted butter
100g baby onions, peeled
100g button mushrooms, stalks
    trimmed if necessary
coarsely chopped fresh flat-leaf parsley
    to serve

Serves 3

Preheat the oven to 170°C fan/190°C/gas mark 5. Heat the oil over a medium-high heat in a casserole that will hold the guinea fowl pieces snugly in a single layer. Season the pieces and colour on both sides. Remove them to a bowl, add the bacon and stir until it just begins to colour. Return the guinea fowl to the casserole, sprinkle over the flour and cook, turning the pieces, for about 1 minute. Pour over the red wine and stock, and add the bay leaf and thyme. Heat the liquid until it just begins to bubble, then cover the casserole with a lid and cook in the oven for 50 minutes, basting the guinea fowl halfway through.

On removing the casserole from the oven, melt the butter in a small frying pan over a low heat. Cook the onions for 10 minutes, turning them frequently, adding the mushrooms a few minutes before the end. They should all be lightly golden and tender. In the meantime, carefully skim any fat off the surface of the casserole. Add the mushrooms and onions, and serve straight away on warm plates, sprinkled with chopped parsley, or transfer to a serving dish.

* The guinea fowl you buy in supermarkets will come whole. They can be jointed in exactly the same way as a chicken, into 8 pieces consisting of breast, thigh, drumstick and wing. If you are handy with a cleaver you can do this yourself; alternatively ask the butcher.

meat

The comfort factor in this chapter is provided by casseroles and stews, with morsels of meat so tender they fall apart at the touch of a fork, sitting in a thick, golden gravy. These are central to British cookery (even if we do borrow heavily from France). They're ones for dishing up over a mound of buttery mash, with a simple and hearty serving of veg – a big bowl of skinny beans with plenty of salty butter, sautéd Savoy cabbage or glazed carrots. And while they aren't meals to rustle up in thirty minutes after work, nor are they very arduous, and especially good for all those of us who work at home. You can take a break late afternoon and have a little potter in the kitchen, and then get back to work for an hour or two while the casserole is in the oven doing its stuff.

I tend to reserve full-on roasts for weekends, but am very fond of a traybake mid-week – an all-in-one dish based on small cuts, like chops. The idea here is that all the components of a roast – the meat, the veggies and potatoes – come out of the oven at the same time, baked to a sticky golden finish in a tray. There's no gravy involved, but you can throw in whole garlic cloves, bay leaves, some lemon zest or chillies for added colour and thrill, and maybe dollop some mayo or an apple sauce over them.

But many is the supper when all you feel like is a nice bit of junk. A juicy burger, a kebab perhaps or some sausages. The good news is that none of these foods are unhealthy in themselves, it's how they're put together and served that makes the difference. In fact, burgers have the potential to be positively healthy, and by grilling them you can take it even further. Dish them up with a little salad of tomatoes, olives and leafy herbs and you can go to bed with a clear conscience. We are also very partial to 'Lulu' kebabs in our house. They are something like a hamburger on a stick, yummily tucked into warm cushions of flatbread. They're great for eating in the garden, and equally good chucked onto the barbecue.

Here are all the good things about a cassoulet without the complication or heaviness. The lamb gently cooks in its own juices, which are then soaked up by the beans, while the merguez provide all the spice you need. Serve a very simple green veg alongside, nothing fancy, some buttery braised marrow or courgettes, broccoli or something leafy like watercress.

strains of cassoulet

extra virgin olive oil

1.2kg lamb shoulder, cut into
   5cm cubes

sea salt, black pepper

6 merguez sausages

2 onions, peeled, halved and
   thinly sliced

3 garlic cloves, peeled and
   finely chopped

1 bay leaf

a couple of sprigs of fresh thyme

150ml white wine

100g dried haricot beans, soaked
   overnight and drained

125g slightly stale sourdough bread
   (weight excluding crusts)

Serves 6

Heat 1 tablespoon of oil in a large cast-iron casserole over a medium heat. Add some of the cubed meat, leaving plenty of space between the pieces, season and sear on all sides, then remove and cook the remainder in the same fashion. Now colour the sausages, then cover these and set aside in a cool place.

Add another tablespoon of oil to the pan if necessary, then add the onions and fry for about 5 minutes, stirring occasionally until golden, adding the garlic and herbs just before the end. Return the lamb to the pan, add the wine, bring to the boil, cover and simmer over a very low heat for 1½ hours, by which time the meat should be almost completely submerged in juices. Check it occasionally and give it a stir.

While the lamb is cooking, bring a medium-size pan of water to the boil. Add the beans and simmer for 30 minutes. Pour out some of the water, and refill with cold water to stop the cooking process.

When the cooking time is up, drain the beans, stir them into the casserole, and add the sausages. Cover and cook for another 30 minutes, then skim off any excess fat. I cooking the casserole in advance, leave to cool, then chill, and then remove the fat.

Preheat the oven to 180°C fan/200°C/gas mark 6. Whiz the bread to coarse crumbs in a food processor, transfer them to a bowl, toss with 3 tablespoons of olive oil and scatter over the casserole. Cook for 40 minutes, until the crumbs are golden and crisp. It may need a little longer if you have chilled it first.

As we all know, the best bit of a Lancashire hotpot is the crispy potatoes on top, so combine them with chipolatas and you have a winning supper. Look out for the Cumberland version of this sausage in the shops. A bunch of watercress can be put to good use.

chipolata and shallot hotpot

3 tablespoons extra virgin
   olive oil
600g chipolatas
300g shallots, peeled
1 tablespoon plain flour
200ml red wine
300ml chicken stock (see page
   31)
1 bay leaf
sea salt, black pepper
500g medium maincrop potatoes,
   peeled and thinly sliced

Serves 4

Preheat the oven to 180°C fan/200°C/gas mark 6. Heat 1 tablespoon of oil in a large frying pan over a medium heat and colour half the sausages on both sides. Remove them to a bowl. Add the remaining sausages to the pan and colour these also. Transfer these to the bowl with the others.

Heat 1 tablespoon of oil in a 30 x 20cm roasting dish over a medium heat, add the shallots and fry until tinged with gold. Sprinkle over the flour and stir, then pour over the red wine and chicken stock. Add the sausages, bay leaf and a little seasoning, and bring to the boil.

Toss the potato slices in a bowl with 1 tablespoon of oil, and lay them on top of the sausages, overlapping in rows like roof tiles. Season them and bake for 40 minutes, until the potatoes are lovely and crisp. Serve straight away.

This is a whiz-bang guacamole that's great served as a little dip, but also has a particularly affinity with tender lamb chops – together a small but sweet treat mid-week.

rack of lamb with guacamole

Lamb

sea salt, black pepper
2 chined racks of lamb
(7–8 cutlets each)
extra virgin olive oil
3–4 unpeeled garlic cloves
a few sprigs of fresh thyme
sliced tomatoes, red
onion slivers and coarsely
chopped fresh coriander
to serve

Guacamole

4 avocados, halved
1 tablespoon chopped red
onion
2 tablespoons lemon juice
Tabasco

Serves 4–6

Preheat the oven to 200°C fan/220°C/gas mark 7. Season the lamb and colour it in a little oil in a roasting dish (don't worry about the ends). Roast on top of the garlic cloves, thyme sprigs and the chine bones if you have them, for 20–25 minutes. Loosely cover with foil and leave to rest for 15 minutes.

Whiz the avocado flesh in a food processor with the red onion, a couple of tablespoons of extra virgin olive oil and the lemon juice, and a shake or two of Tabasco.

Carve the racks into chops. Serve with the guacamole, scattered with sliced cocktail tomatoes and slivers of red onion, with a little more oil and some chopped coriander.

A virtuous line-up that many a diet guru would give the nod to. Some may like to forgo the stodge of a bun, but some warm pitta bread goes down well. Using the same method you could also make a fine beef burger – with minced beef, chopped shallots and a little chopped parsley.

lamb burgers
with herb relish

Burgers

450g minced lamb
1 tablespoon finely chopped shallots
2 teaspoons ground cumin
1 teaspoon ground coriander
¼ teaspoon ground cinnamon
¼ teaspoon ground allspice
sea salt, black pepper

Relish

1 beefsteak tomato
1 large handful of fresh mint leaves,
    coarsely chopped
1 large handful of fresh flat-leaf
    parsley leaves, coarsely chopped
75g black olives, pitted and
    coarsely chopped
a squeeze of lemon juice

Serves 4

Blend all the ingredients for the burgers in a bowl, mixing thoroughly with a wooden spoon to distribute the spices evenly. Take a quarter of the mixture at a time and shape it into a ball, then flatten it into a burger 10cm in diameter. You can make the burgers in advance, cover and chill them.

Cut out a cone from the top of the tomato to remove the core, plunge it into boiling water for 20 seconds and then into cold water. Quarter, remove the seeds and dice the flesh.

Preheat a ridged griddle over a medium-low heat or a conventional grill on a high heat. Combine all the ingredients for the herb relish in a bowl and season. Cook the burgers for 4–5 minutes each side and serve with some of the relish on top.

Few of us need convincing of the attraction of pies, and this is a really luxurious take on a cottage pie, where slowly braised beef in a red wine gravy is topped with mash and crispy breadcrumbs. You get lashings of extra gravy to boot.

a meaty potato pie with red wine and onion gravy

Beef

150ml medium sherry
2 garlic cloves, peeled and
    crushed to a paste
a few sprigs of fresh thyme
1 bay leaf, torn into pieces
1kg chuck steak, cut into 2cm dice
extra virgin olive oil
600g onions, peeled, halved
    and sliced
1 bottle of red wine
sea salt, black pepper

Mash

1.3kg maincrop potatoes, peeled
    and halved or quartered if large
120g unsalted butter, diced
3 tablespoons milk
1 tablespoon Dijon mustard
50g white breadcrumbs

Serves 6

Combine the sherry, garlic, thyme and bay leaf in a large bowl. Add the meat and baste it, then cover and chill for about 6 hours or overnight, basting it again halfway through.

Remove the meat from the marinade (reserve this) and drain it on a double layer of kitchen paper. Heat 1 tablespoon of olive oil in a large frying pan over a high heat, and sear the meat a little at a time so as not to overcrowd the pan, adding more oil as necessary.

Heat a couple of tablespoons of oil in a large casserole over a medium-high heat, add the onions, and cook for 10–15 minutes until golden. Add the reserved marinade, the wine and some seasoning, and then the beef. Bring to the boil, cover and cook over a low heat for 2 hours, giving it a stir halfway through. Transfer the meat and most of the onions to a bowl, discarding the herbs, and add just enough of the gravy to moisten it.

About halfway through cooking the beef, bring a large pan of salted water to the boil. Add the potatoes and simmer until tender. Drain and leave for a minute or two to steam dry, then pass through a mouli-légumes back into the pan. Add the butter, and once this has melted add the milk, the mustard and plenty of seasoning.

Preheat the oven to 180°C fan/200°C/gas mark 6. Spoon the meat into a shallow baking dish or a 20 x 30cm roasting pan, smooth the potato on top, and fork the surface into furrows. Toss the breadcrumbs with 1 tablespoon of oil, scatter over, and bake for 35–40 minutes. Reheat and serve the remaining red wine gravy alongside.

Steak has a call of its own, and there are times when only a big juicy piece of red meat hits the spot. I prefer green peppercorns here to black – they provide the necessary rasp without the intense heat. The obvious sides are a pile of lightly dressed salad leaves and crispy sautéd potatoes laced with garlic and parsley.

steak 'au poivre'

2 tablespoons green peppercorns in
  brine, rinsed
2 x 175g fillet steaks, 2–3cm thick
sea salt
1 tablespoon extra virgin olive oil
25g unsalted butter, diced
a generous slug of brandy

Serves 2

Coarsely chop the peppercorns on a board. Spread them out in a thin layer, season the steak with salt and press each side into the peppercorns to sparsely coat it. Heat the olive oil in a frying pan over a medium heat and cook the steak for 3 minutes, then add the butter, which will fizzle. Turn the steak and cook it for another 3 minutes on the other side. Don't expect the peppercorns to cling in quite the same way as black and white ones; any that fall off will turn nicely golden and crunchy. Remove the steak to a plate to rest for a few minutes.

Standing well back in case it ignites, add the brandy to the pan. Once this stops seething cook it for a moment longer, scraping up any caramelised bits on the bottom. Serve the steak with the juices spooned over.

It's fillet steak for a treat, and to justify it at least you don't need quite as much as a rump or sirloin, but equally other cuts will do here.

fillet steak with caramelised shallots and orange wedges

600g shallots, peeled and halved
1 orange, cut into 8 wedges
3–4 tablespoons extra virgin olive oil
1 tablespoon dark muscovado sugar
4 x 150g fillet steaks, 2–3cm thick
sea salt, black pepper
25g unsalted butter, diced
3 tablespoons port or Madeira
4 teaspoons sour cream and coarsely
   chopped fresh flat-leaf parsley to serve

Serves 4

Preheat the oven to 170°C fan/190°C/gas mark 5. Arrange the shallots and orange wedges in a roasting dish that holds them snugly in a single layer. Drizzle over 2 tablespoons of olive oil, scatter over the sugar and roast for 45 minutes until golden and caramelised, basting them halfway through.

Ten minutes before the shallots are ready, heat 1 tablespoon of oil in a large frying pan over a medium heat. If your frying pan isn't large enough to hold all the steaks, use two, adding 1 tablespoon of oil to each one. Season the steaks with salt and pepper and cook for 2–3 minutes, then add the butter, which will fizzle. Turn the steaks and cook for another 2–3 minutes on the other side to leave them medium-rare – they should still feel slightly soft when you press them. Remove the steak to a plate to rest for a few minutes. Skim off most of the fat from one of the pans, add the port or Madeira and simmer until well reduced. Add any juices given out by the steak.

Place the steak on warmed plates with the juices spooned over, accompanied by the shallots (I leave the orange in for colour). Dollop a spoonful of sour cream on top of each steak and scatter with parsley.

lulu kebabs with tzatziki

Select eight 20cm skewers. If using wooden skewers, soak them first for 10 minutes in cold water. Combine all the ingredients for the kebabs with 1½ teaspoons of salt and some black pepper, using your hands, then divide the mixture into 8 balls the size of a small apple. Shape each one of these into a long, flat sausage 10–12cm in length and about 3cm wide, and slip a skewer lengthwise through the middle so the tip is just concealed by the end of the kebab. Set these aside on a plate. They can be made up to 24 hours in advance, in which case cover and chill them.

To make the tzatziki, blend the yoghurt with 2 tablespoons of olive oil, the lemon juice, garlic, mint, sugar and a little seasoning in a bowl. Peel the cucumber, slit it in half lengthways and scoop out the seeds, using a teaspoon. Now slice it into half-moons and stir these into the yoghurt mixture. Taste to check the seasoning, then pile it into a clean bowl and pour over a little olive oil. This can be made up to a couple of hours in advance, in which case cover and set it aside somewhere cool.

outdoors To cook the kebabs, barbecue them for 15–20 minutes in total, turning them as necessary and cooking them on all four sides.

indoors Heat a ridged griddle over a medium-high heat and grill the kebabs for about 15 minutes in all, cooking them on all four sides. You may need to cook them in batches.

Serve the kebabs with the tzatziki.

Kebabs

700g minced lamb
1 shallot, peeled and finely chopped
2 tablespoons finely chopped fresh
  flat-leaf parsley
½ teaspoon each ground cumin,
  cinnamon and nutmeg
sea salt, black pepper

Tzatziki

250g Greek yoghurt
extra virgin olive oil
1 teaspoon lemon juice
1 garlic clove, peeled and crushed
  to a paste
2 tablespoons finely sliced fresh mint
a large pinch of caster sugar
1 cucumber

Makes 8

These spicy hamburgers on sticks are a big favourite with children, and great barbecue material. I quite often keep a few in the freezer – they defrost within the hour at the ready to grill for supper. The tzatziki allows for a tablespoon per person, so if serving it as the main salad you could double the quantity.

A working man's pie that's full of class, this one spans all ages and occasions. But it's most at home at a family supper with a big bottle of tomato ketchup.

shepherd's pie

1.3kg maincrop potatoes, peeled
and halved or quartered if large
120g unsalted butter, diced, plus
an extra knob
3 tablespoons milk
sea salt, black pepper
2 tablespoons vegetable oil

3 shallots, peeled and chopped
1 large or 2 small carrots, peeled
and thinly sliced
1 leek, trimmed, halved and thinly
sliced
1 bay leaf
2 sprigs of fresh thyme

900g minced lamb
150ml red wine
2 tablespoons tomato ketchup
1 teaspoon Worcestershire sauce
150g frozen petits pois

Serves 6

Bring a large pan of salted water to the boil. Add the potatoes and simmer until tender. Drain them into a sieve or a colander and leave for a minute or two for any surface moisture to evaporate, then pass through a mouli-légumes or a sieve back into the pan. Add the 120g of butter, and once this has melted add the milk and plenty of seasoning.

At the same time, prepare the mince. Heat the oil in a medium-size saucepan and cook the vegetables and herbs gently for about 8 minutes over a low heat until glossy and tender. Add the minced lamb, turn the heat up and cook, stirring occasionally, until it changes colour and separates. Add all the remaining ingredients except the peas, including some seasoning, bring to a simmer and cook over a low heat for 15 minutes, adding the peas after 10 minutes. There should still be plenty of juices, but skim off any excess fat. Transfer the mince to a shallow ovenproof dish or a 20 x 30cm roasting pan, discarding the herbs. Smooth the potato on top and fork the surface into furrows. You can prepare the pie to this point in advance, in which case leave it to cool, then cover and chill.

Preheat the oven to 180°C fan/200°C/gas mark 6, dot the surface with butter and cook for 35–40 minutes.

Lamb shanks work beautifully in a 'rogan josh', demanding a long slow cooking and emerging succulent and infused with the spices. Hearty male appetites might be able to cope with one lamb shank each, but otherwise three or four between six will be ample.

lamb shanks 'rogan josh'

2 heaped tablespoons tomato purée
a pinch of saffron filaments
   (approx. 20)
1 heaped teaspoon paprika
¾ teaspoon cayenne pepper
2 tablespoons groundnut
   or vegetable oil
sea salt, black pepper
3–4 lamb shanks, depending on size
3 onions, peeled, halved and sliced
3 garlic cloves, peeled and
   finely chopped
2 teaspoons garam masala
1 heaped teaspoon cumin
1 heaped teaspoon turmeric
2 bay leaves
chopped fresh coriander and warm
   naan bread to serve

Serves 4–6

Place the tomato purée, saffron, paprika and cayenne pepper in a small bowl and gradually blend in 300ml of water.

Heat the oil in a large casserole over a medium-high heat. Season the lamb shanks and colour them all over, then remove them to a bowl. Turn the heat down, add the onions and fry for 5–7 minutes, until lightly golden, stirring frequently, and adding the garlic just before the end. Stir in the garam masala, cumin and turmeric, and then the tomato purée mixture and the bay leaves. Return the lamb shanks to the casserole, add some salt, bring to the boil, cover and simmer over a low heat for 2 hours, turning the shanks halfway through and giving the sauce a stir to make sure it isn't sticking.

Transfer the lamb shanks to a bowl and loosely cover with foil to keep warm. Leave the juices to settle for about 5 minutes and then skim off the fat. The remaining juices should be rich and thick, so if they seem at all thin bring them back to the boil and simmer to reduce by about a third. Taste for seasoning. Serve the lamb shanks with the sauce spooned over, scattered with coriander and accompanied by warm naan bread.

You may have some spicy little sauce in the cupboard that will take the place of the mint harissa, something with a little bite to it. I would also serve a simple salad of rocket leaves with this.

lamb and potato traybake with mint harissa

Traybake

1.2kg small new potatoes, scrubbed
   if necessary but not peeled,
   and halved
1 lemon, halved and sliced,
   ends discarded
6 bay leaves
2 tablespoons extra virgin olive oil
40g unsalted butter
sea salt, black pepper
8 lamb loin chops
coarsely chopped fresh coriander
   to serve

Harissa

1 orange (or red) pepper
a handful of fresh mint leaves
3 tablespoons extra virgin olive oil
1–3 teaspoons harissa

Serves 4

Preheat the oven to 190°C fan/210°C/gas mark 6. Arrange the potatoes, lemon slices and bay leaves on the base of a 38 x 25cm roasting dish. Drizzle over the olive oil, dot with the butter and season. Cover with foil and roast for 25 minutes. Remove the foil from the roasting dish, give the potatoes a stir and roast for another 30 minutes.

About 10 minutes before the end of this time, heat a large frying pan over a high heat. Season the chops and colour on both sides, also the fat – you will need to do this in two batches. Tuck the chops in between the potatoes and roast for another 15 minutes. Serve the chops and potatoes scattered with coriander, accompanied by the mint harissa.

At the same time as putting the potatoes in to roast, cook the pepper on the oven rack for 25 minutes, then remove and leave to cool. This will mean finishing the sauce just before you eat, but you can if you prefer roast the pepper and make the sauce in advance.

Skin and deseed the pepper, then whiz the flesh in a food processor with the mint, olive oil, a little salt and the harissa. Add this to taste – there is a huge difference in the strength of commercial harissas. Authentic tubes are very much hotter than commercial brands, so start with a teaspoon and work upwards.

All sorts of goodies are added here to bring your pork chops to life – lemon, Parmesan and crispy parsnips. The apple relish is a frill; if you have a good jar of apple sauce at the back of the fridge this will do nicely.

pork, parsnip and lemon traybake

Traybake

1.2kg parsnips, trimmed, peeled and
   halved or quartered lengthwise, cut
   into 2 shorter lengths if long
1 lemon, cut into slim wedges
4 tablespoons extra virgin olive oil
sea salt, black pepper
4 rindless pork loin chops, 2cm thick
75g shaved Parmesan

Relish

5 tablespoons extra virgin olive oil
1 stick of celery heart, finely diced
½ eating apple, peeled, cored and
   finely diced
2 teaspoons balsamic vinegar
a pinch of golden caster sugar
sea salt, black pepper
10g fresh basil leaves, finely chopped
10g fresh mint leaves, finely chopped

Serves 4

Preheat the oven to 190°C fan/210°C/gas mark 6. Bring a large pan of salted water to the boil. Add the parsnips and cook for 6 minutes, then drain into a colander and leave for a few minutes to steam dry. Return the parsnips to the saucepan with the lemon wedges, add the olive oil and some seasoning and toss. Arrange in a roasting pan (about 38 x 25cm) and roast for 35 minutes, stirring once, until well on the way to being golden.

Meanwhile, make the apple and herb relish. Heat 1 tablespoon of the oil in a large frying pan over a high heat, and cook the celery and apple for a few minutes until softened, stirring occasionally. Leave to cool, then whisk the vinegar with the sugar and some seasoning. Whisk in the remaining oil and stir in the herbs, and the apple and celery.

Halfway through cooking the parsnips, heat a large non-stick frying pan over a high heat. Season the chops and colour well on both sides, then turn them on their sides to colour the fat as well. You will need to do this in two batches, reserving them on a plate as you go.

Stir the Parmesan into the parsnips, then tuck in the chops so some of the vegetables and cheese cover them, and pour over any juices given out by the meat. Roast for another 10 minutes. Leave to stand for 5 minutes, then discard the lemon and serve the chops and parsnips with the juices spooned over, accompanied by the relish.

This is a really good classic beef stew, lightened with sautéd wild mushrooms at the very end, but these could just as well be button or other cultivated types — being supper it doesn't have to spell luxury. The crisp wafers of French bread should go a long way to ensure you feel indulged, but equally you could ladle it over buttery spuds or rice, cooking it until the beef is tender.

steak and wild mushroom carbonade

50g unsalted butter, plus extra
   for spreading
3 onions, peeled, halved and sliced
3 garlic cloves, peeled
900g chuck steak, cut into 4cm dice
2 tablespoons plain flour
sea salt, black pepper
150ml Madeira
600ml beef stock
2 tablespoons extra virgin olive oil
250g wild mushrooms, trimmed and
   sliced if necessary
approx. 20 thin slices of French bread
   (about half a baguette)
coarsely chopped fresh flat-leaf parsley
   to serve

Serves 4

Preheat the oven to 160°C fan/180°C/gas mark 4. Melt half the butter in a large cast-iron casserole over a medium heat, add the onions, and fry for 8–10 minutes until golden, stirring them occasionally. Smash 2 of the garlic cloves with the end of a rolling pin and add them just before the end. Remove the vegetables to a bowl. Toss the beef with the flour and some seasoning in another bowl, and seal it in two batches, adding half the remaining butter with each one. You may need to turn the heat up towards the end. Return the onions to the casserole, pour over the Madeira and beef stock, and add some seasoning. Bring the liquid to the boil, then cover and cook in the oven for 1½ hours.

Remove the casserole and turn the oven up to 180°C fan/200°C/gas mark 6. Sauté the mushrooms in two lots — it's important not to overcrowd the pan. Heat 1 tablespoon of oil in a large frying pan over a high heat, add half the mushrooms and toss them constantly until they are soft, seasoning them towards the end. If any liquid is given out in the process, keep cooking until it evaporates. Add the mushrooms to the casserole and cook the remainder likewise, then add these too. Season the stew to taste.

Liberally rub one side of the slices of French bread with the remaining garlic clove, cut in half, and spread the other side with the rest of the butter. Arrange the bread slices so they overlap, garlic side down, in rows on top of the casserole and return to the oven for another 30–40 minutes, until they are golden and crisp. Serve straight away, scattering a little parsley over the beef and mushrooms.

It was a neighbour in France, Arthur Higgo, who taught me this brilliant South African way with sausages in a sticky tomato sauce. Apart from producing deliciously caramelised bangers, when barbecuing the grill is freed up for 30 minutes at the end, leaving you plenty of space to grill whatever else is lined up. If you are cooking for any number, this is a real plus. Though they can be cooked indoors too.

arthur's way
with sausages

3 tablespoons extra virgin olive oil
2 onions, peeled, halved and finely
    sliced
5 garlic cloves, peeled and finely
    chopped
1½ teaspoons light muscovado sugar
100ml white wine
2 x 400g tins of chopped plum
    tomatoes
sea salt, black pepper
1.3kg chunky bangers

Serves 6

Heat the olive oil in a medium-size saucepan over a medium-low heat and fry the onions for 10–12 minutes, stirring frequently, until lightly caramelised. Add the garlic and cook for a minute or two longer, again stirring frequently as the onions will caramelise quite quickly at this point.

Add the sugar and stir, then add the wine and simmer to reduce by half. Add the tomatoes and some seasoning, bring to a simmer and cook over a medium-low heat for 25–30 minutes, until well-reduced and thick, stirring now and again especially towards the end. Spoon the sauce into a large cast-iron roasting tray that will hold the sausages in a single layer.

outdoors Preheat the oven to 180°C fan/200°C/gas mark 6. Barbecue the sausages for 15–25 minutes until nicely caramelised without being fully cooked, turning them every so often to ensure they colour evenly. Arrange them on top of the tomato sauce, spooning some of it over. Roast for 25–30 minutes, basting them halfway through. The sauce by the end should be caramelised at the edges, and the sausages deep gold and sticky.

indoors Heat a little olive oil in a large frying pan over a medium heat and slowly colour the sausages on all sides, for 20–25 minutes. Try to do this as evenly as possible, turning them frequently; they should by the end be a nice golden colour. You will need to fry them in two batches. Proceed to cook them in the oven in the tomato sauce as above.

veg

As a dedicated veg-o-phile, I cannot think of a single one that I don't like. Well, maybe okra, which oozes a slimy substance that could for all its strangeness come from outer space. But otherwise there isn't a vegetable out there I wouldn't happily eat by the plateful. That said, they are not all born equal. There is an A-list whose members lend themselves to being eaten on their own or as the star of a dish, when they are positively sumptuous.

Uniting this select group are exquisite textures and flavours. The likes of mushrooms, onions, aubergines and tomatoes take on a different dimension when given the chance to go golden at the edges. Among the simplest vegetables to bake or roast are large, floppy flat-cap mushrooms that invite you to fill them with garlic, lemon and chilli – they come out of the oven dripping with dark juices, and it's in there with a toothsome crust of bread. Chicory too calls for little – tossed with olive oil and snippets of blue cheese, and some dried figs to offset the bitter and salty character, it emerges a silky, gooey mass.

Courgettes are one of my favourite vegetable basket staples, not least because they last for ages, at the ready to be grilled and dipped into a toasted almond sauce or scattered with chopped herbs and eaten with fresh goat's cheese or ricotta. And aubergines can be sliced and roasted and lend themselves to any number of ways of dressing up. But the most modest standby, and one for which it's almost worth finding yourself alone of an evening in order to indulge, is grilled tomatoes, soft and sweet on a piece of hot buttered toast. And if you do have company and that seems too back to the nursery, they can be dished up in other guises, baked in a red pepper shell with a drizzle of honey or spread with a thick herb crust and grilled.

No more complicated than tossing a salad, this is a great standby, and it also makes a fine starter if you're running to that. Ideally use a mixture of red and white chicory here, for two-tone colour. And use whatever half packet of dried fruit is taking up cupboard space – I haven't tried it with apricots or prunes but I'm sure it would be scrumptious.

oven-roast chicory with blue cheese and figs

9 heads of chicory
4 tablespoons extra virgin olive oil
225g Stilton or Roquefort, diced
9 dried figs, stalks trimmed,
   thinly sliced

A little extra
6 slices of Parma ham

Serves 4

Heat the oven to 220°C fan/240°C/gas mark 9. Trim the base of the chicory heads, discard any damaged outer leaves, and separate out the leaves. Toss these in a bowl with the olive oil, and gently mix in the blue cheese and figs. Tip into a large 38 x 25cm roasting dish and roast for 8–10 minutes, until the chicory is golden on top and the cheese melted and gooey.

Five minutes before you put the chicory in to cook, lay the ham out on one or two baking sheets (it looks prettiest if you halve it lengthwise first) and pop it into the oven for 3–4 minutes until it appears ruched at the edges and darker in colour. Remove from the oven and turn the slices over – they will crisp up while the chicory is cooking. Serve on top of the chicory and cheese.

This delectably simple way of cooking flat-cap mushrooms is apt with any roast or grilled meat, bacon and fried eggs, or alone with some crusty bread for mopping up all the inky mushroom juices.

mushrooms baked with garlic, lemon and chilli

8 medium flat-cap mushrooms

2–4 garlic cloves, peeled and
   finely chopped

1 medium-hot fresh red chilli, core
   and seeds removed, finely chopped

grated zest of 1 lemon,
   plus 1 tablespoon of juice

3 tablespoons extra virgin olive oil

25g unsalted butter

sea salt, black pepper

2 tablespoons coarsely chopped
   fresh flat-leaf parsley

Serves 4

Preheat the oven to 180°C fan/200°C/gas mark 6. Trim the ends of the mushroom stalks and arrange the mushrooms in a roasting dish, cup side up. Divide the garlic, chilli and lemon zest between the cups. Drizzle over the olive oil, dot with the butter, season and bake for 25 minutes.

When they come out of the oven, sprinkle the lemon juice over the mushrooms and scatter with the parsley. Serve hot or warm.

Stuffing onions is a tearful chore, not something to take on after a hard day's work, but this deconstructed version is that much friendlier, and yummier to boot.

gratin of onions with goat's cheese and thyme

4 onions, peeled and cut into 8
  wedges
extra virgin olive oil
50g white breadcrumbs
150g goat's cheese (e.g. chèvre log),
  rind removed, diced
1 teaspoon fresh thyme leaves

Serves 4

Preheat the oven to 180°C fan/200°C/gas mark 6. Lay the onion wedges in a baking dish pointed side up, so they fit quite snugly. Drizzle about 3 tablespoons of oil over, and roast for 40 minutes, basting halfway through.

Toss the breadcrumbs with a couple of tablespoons of oil. Scatter the goat's cheese, breadcrumbs and thyme over the onions, drizzle over a little more oil and bake for another 20 minutes. Serve hot or cold.

There's very little vegetarian food that offers the ease of chucking a chicken breast on to the grill. This, however, is an exception to the rule: you can prepare it in advance and pop the squash into the oven half an hour before you want to eat. The combination of squash and melted cheese is unfailingly sensational and you could provide salty butter as an extra for those that want it.

fondue-filled butternut squash

Fondue

1 tablespoon kirsch or white wine
1 tablespoon cornflour
130g Gruyère, grated
40g crème fraîche
sea salt, black pepper
freshly grated nutmeg

Squash

2 butternut squash (approx. 700g each)
1 garlic clove, peeled and crushed to a paste
1 tablespoon fresh thyme leaves
25g unsalted butter, melted
croûtons (optional; see page 30)

Serves 4

Preheat the oven to 190°C fan/210°C/gas mark 6. Blend the kirsch or wine with the cornflour in a bowl, then add the remaining ingredients for the fondue and work to a paste, using a spoon. Halve the squash lengthwise – I find it easiest to first slice through the bulb, then turn the squash stalk down and cut through the trunk. Scoop out the seeds and fibrous matter from each half using a teaspoon, and score the flesh of the trunk in a criss-cross pattern at 2cm intervals, using the tip of a sharp knife.

Divide the crushed garlic between the squash hollows and, using your fingers, smear it over the surface. Fill the cavities with the fondue paste to within a couple of millimetres of the surface – there should be a little room left for the cheese to bubble without overflowing. The squash can be prepared to this point in advance, in which case heat the oven just before cooking.

It's important that the squash bake level in order to contain the fondue within the hollows. Arrange the squash halves top to tail in a roasting dish, using foil loosely bundled into a ball to raise the thin end of the trunk to the same level as the bulb. Season the surface of the squash, scatter over the thyme and drizzle with the melted butter. Bake the squash for 35–45 minutes, until the fondue is golden and bubbling and the trunk of the squash is tender when pierced with a knife. Serve straight away, accompanied by croûtons if wished.

I am more likely to turn to orange-fleshed sweet potatoes than classic jackets for a workaday supper; their sweetness heralds other big flavours like lemon, sage and chilli. This is half vegetable dish and half salad – either way it's good relaxed stuff.

roast sweet potato mélange

extra virgin olive oil
4 orange-fleshed sweet potatoes
   (approx. 175g each), washed
10g sage leaves
1 medium-hot fresh red chilli,
   core, seeds and membranes
   removed
4 handfuls of rocket
sea salt
½ lemon, cut into 4 wedges

Serves 4

Preheat the oven to 200°C fan/220°C/gas mark 7. Pour a little oil into the palm of your hand, then rub your hands together and lightly coat each sweet potato. Place the potatoes in a small roasting dish and cook in the oven for 30 minutes, until tender. Remove and leave them to cool.

Heat 3–4mm of olive oil in a large frying pan over a medium heat – it should be hot enough to immerse a cube of bread in bubbles. Carefully scatter the sage leaves over the surface; they will bubble and fizz as the heat of the oil drives off the moisture. Once this subsides, remove them using a slotted spoon and drain on kitchen paper. Leave them to cool.

Slip the skins off the potatoes and cut them into slices about 2cm thick. Lay these out on a plate. Finely slice the red chilli flesh and, if long, halve the strips – they should be about 3cm in length. Scatter these over the potatoes, and add the sage leaves.

To serve, pile the potatoes on to four plates, lifting them gently as they will be soft and comparatively fragile. Place a pile of rocket leaves on top, drizzle over a little olive oil and season with a pinch of salt. Serve with lemon wedges.

Grilling courgettes has to be their finest hour – they emerge from the grill an entirely different vegetable from their raw and austere selves, turning sweet and luscious. Use this as a basic and embellish it with whatever tasty bits and pieces you have to hand: slivers of Parmesan, slow-roasted tomatoes, goat's cheese and the like.

grilled courgettes with almond sauce

Courgettes

4 courgettes, ends removed,
    cut into long thin strips
extra virgin olive oil
sea salt, black pepper
3 spring onions, trimmed and thinly
    sliced diagonally
75g black olives, pitted
paprika

Sauce

65g flaked almonds
3 garlic cloves, peeled and chopped
50g day-old coarse-textured white
    bread (weight excluding crusts)
2 teaspoons red wine or sherry vinegar

Serves 4

Heat a ridged griddle over a medium-high heat. Take as many courgette strips as will fit the griddle, brush them with olive oil on one side and season. Grill this side for 3–5 minutes, until striped with gold, then brush the tops, turn and grill this side too. Remove the strips to a plate and grill the remainder in the same fashion, then leave to cool. You can cook the courgettes well in advance.

To prepare the sauce, whiz 50g of the almonds with the garlic in a food processor to a coarse meal. Briefly soak the bread in water, squeeze it dry, add it to the food processor and whiz again. With the motor running, gradually add 10 tablespoons of olive oil and the vinegar, and season with salt. Add the rest of the almonds and briefly whiz again. (I like to toast them in a frying pan first for about 5 minutes, stirring occasionally, until lightly golden, but this isn't essential.) Transfer the sauce to a bowl.

Shortly before eating, scatter the spring onions and olives over the courgettes, drizzle over a little more oil and dust with paprika. Serve with the almond sauce.

The texture of this one has me weak at the knees, a winning combination of meltingly tender aubergine and gooey mozzarella, with a tomato sauce and piquant green olives. Full of big Riviera flavours, and not hard to imagine settling down in the shade of an umbrella pine to the song of cicadas.

aubergine gratin with mozzarella and olives

3–4 medium aubergines
extra virgin olive oil
sea salt, black pepper
250ml tomato passata*, seasoned with
  salt and pepper
2 x 125g buffalo mozzarellas, drained
  and sliced
75g green olives, pitted and halved
50g freshly grated Parmesan

Serves 6

Preheat the oven to 180°C fan/200°C/gas mark 6. Removing the stalk from each aubergine, slice them lengthwise 1cm thick. Heat a large dry frying pan, or even better two. Brush one side of each aubergine slice with oil, season and fry this side until golden. Brush the tops with oil, then turn and grill this side too. As the slices are cooked, arrange them in overlapping rows in a 30 x 20cm gratin dish.

Having covered the base with half the aubergine slices, spoon over half the passata, lay over half the mozzarella and scatter over all the olives. Now repeat with the remaining aubergine slices. Spoon over the rest of the passata, lay the remaining mozzarella over and scatter over the Parmesan. Bake for 25–30 minutes, until nicely golden and gooey. Serve hot or warm. The gratin can be successfully reheated for 20–25 minutes in a medium oven, though the mozzarella will never return to being quite as gooey.

* Look out for sugocasa, even better than passata, a chopped tomato sauce that has a good chunky texture. Alternatively you could briefly whiz tinned chopped tomatoes in a food processor.

This is the easy way, aubergine slices roasted in the oven until golden and slightly chewy on the outside: they offer little resistance within and there's no hovering over a hot grill. They're eaten with some Middle Eastern charm in the way of a sharp tahini dressing and some pomegranate seeds, and a herby fattoush salad.

grilled aubergine with fattoush

Aubergine

3 medium aubergines, ends discarded,
    cut into 1cm slices
extra virgin olive oil
sea salt, black pepper
2 tablespoons lemon juice
1 garlic clove, peeled and crushed to
    a paste
3 tablespoons tahini
1 pomegranate, seeds removed

Fattoush

3 pitta breads, slit in half
extra virgin olive oil
500g small tomatoes on the vine,
    quartered
sea salt
a pinch of sugar
150g radishes, trimmed and quartered
½ red onion, finely sliced
20g each fresh mint, coriander and
    parsley leaves
1 tablespoon lemon juice

Serves 6

Preheat the oven to 180°C fan/200°C/gas mark 6. Lay the aubergines out on a couple of baking trays, brushing the slices with oil on both sides, and seasoning the top. Roast for 20 minutes, then turn them and cook for another 10–20 minutes until golden (the lower tray may need longer than the top). Loosen with a spatula and leave to cool. Leave the oven turned on.

Meanwhile, make a tahini dressing. Blend the lemon juice with the garlic and a little salt in a bowl, then add the tahini and blend to a thick paste. Add 4 tablespoons of water and whisk. The dressing should be the consistency of double cream, so add a little more water if necessary.

To make the fattoush, lay the pitta halves out on a couple of baking trays and brush them on either side with oil. Once the aubergine slices are out of the oven, bake the pittas for 10–12 minutes, until golden and crisp, removing them as they are ready. Leave to cool, then break into pieces. Place the tomatoes in a large bowl and season with salt and the sugar. Scatter the radishes over, then the onion and herbs, and pile the bread on top. Whisk the lemon juice with a little salt and 3 tablespoons of oil, and when you're ready to serve, pour the dressing over the fattoush and toss.

Arrange the aubergine slices on a plate, drizzling over the tahini dressing and scattering with pomegranate seeds as you go. Serve with the herby fattoush.

salads

Despite having fallen off the vegetarian wagon many years ago, it has never dampened my passion for salads and vegetable dishes. Weeks can go by and I don't even notice that I haven't eaten meat or fish. My husband, however, does notice. One or two evenings without anything red-blooded for supper might just about pass muster, but any longer than this and the cravings set in. Which makes salads such a great meeting place. I can indulge my passion for all things green while dishing up a cold roast, some air-dried ham or salami on the side, and everyone is happy.

I love salads that make a real splash, big plates and over-sized bowls piled high with a mixture of succulent vegetables, leaves, toasted seeds and nuts, cheese and croûtons – a bowl of baby spinach leaves with pomegranate seeds and cubes of feta, or a mélange of fresh peas, mangetouts and sugar-snaps with mint leaves and mozzarella. A basket of crusty breads and flaky pastries and you have the makings of a gorgeous supper.

But equally important are tomato salads and leafy green ones in supporting roles. These will accompany a frittata or other omelette, or simply lend a little respectability to a potato dish. A tomato salad, providing the fruits are juicy and ripe, need involve little more than slicing and seasoning, while a green salad can consist of just one fine leaf – frisée, lamb's lettuce, chicory and floppy green lettuces are all personal favourites.

Almost more important than the leaf is the dressing, which can make or break a salad. The easy way around this is a good olive oil and a squeeze of lemon or some balsamic vinegar, while a French vinaigrette is more of an art and takes that little bit longer. My ideal contains crushed garlic, Dijon mustard, a suspicion of sugar to offset the vinegar, and just a little olive oil mixed with some groundnut oil – as good for dunking crudités or dipping the leaves of an artichoke as it is for a bowl of green leaves.

The allure of this salad is, as much as anything, the legend behind it. So travel back in time to Tijuana, Mexico, in the 1920s, when chef and restaurateur Cesar Cardini had all but run out of food after a weekend spent cooking for a group of Hollywood movie stars. When their departure was delayed one more mealtime, he rustled up a salad with Romaine lettuce, very lightly poached eggs, Worcestershire sauce, garlic, lemon juice, olive oil, grated Parmesan and croûtons. Quite where the anchovies came from is a mystery, and the cause of much debate. I prefer to leave them out if Parmesan is included, but there are no rules. Whichever way you play it, the salad lends itself to endless interpretation – be it slivers of roast chicken, roast peppers, avocado and crisp strips of bacon, or chicory in lieu of the Romaine lettuce, with crumbled Roquefort.

classic caesar

Croûtons

groundnut oil for frying
2 large slices of white bread, 1cm
    thick, crusts removed, diced

Dressing

2 medium eggs
½ garlic clove, peeled and coarsely
    chopped
2 tablespoons lemon juice
2 teaspoons Worcestershire sauce
150ml extra virgin olive oil
sea salt, black pepper

Salad

4 Romaine lettuce hearts
70g freshly grated Parmesan

Serves 4

To prepare the croûtons, heat about 1cm of groundnut oil in a large frying pan over a medium heat until a cube of bread immersed is surrounded by bubbles. Add half the cubes and fry, tossing now and again, until golden and crisp. Transfer them, using a slotted spoon, to a double thickness of kitchen paper and leave to cool. Cook the remainder likewise.

To prepare the dressing, bring a small pan of water to the boil, carefully drop the eggs in and cook for 1 minute, then remove and cool them under cold running water. Shell them into a liquidiser, scooping out the cooked white that lines the inside of the shell. Add the remaining ingredients for the dressing and whiz to a pale and creamy emulsion. The salad can be prepared to this point in advance.

To serve the salad, separate out the lettuce leaves, discarding any outer leathery or blowsy dark green leaves (these can be saved for a soup or purée, or trimmed for slicing into another salad). Arrange the Romaine leaves on two large platters or four dinner plates. Pour over the dressing and scatter over the Parmesan, and finally the croûtons. Serve straight away.

A ray of sunshine in the depth of winter, the cheering red of the pomegranate seeds set against the green of the spinach. Serve with the marinated feta and slices of warmed pitta bread for supper. The salad also goes well with grilled lamb chops.

spinach, feta and pomegranate salad

200g feta, thinly sliced
5 tablespoons extra virgin olive oil
a couple of squeezes of lemon juice
sea salt, black pepper
200g baby spinach leaves
1 tablespoon small fresh mint leaves
4 medium spring onions, trimmed and
    finely sliced diagonally
1 pomegranate, seeds removed

Serves 4

Lay the feta slices out on a large plate, pour over 2 tablespoons of the olive oil and a squeeze of lemon juice and season with black pepper. Cover and chill until required.

Pick over the spinach leaves, wash them in a sink of cold water, then dry them in a salad spinner or, failing that, place them in a clean tea towel, gather up the corners and give it a jolly good shake outside until the showers die out. Put them into a bowl. You can prepare the salad to this point up to an hour in advance.

To serve, pile the feta slices in a bowl with the mint leaves, and pour over any leftover marinade. Drizzle 3 tablespoons of olive oil over the spinach salad and gently toss, using your hands to coat the leaves. Now squeeze over a little lemon juice, scrunch over a few crystals of sea salt, scatter over half the spring onion slices and pomegranate seeds and toss again. Taste a leaf to make sure the leaves are correctly dressed, and scatter over the remaining spring onion and pomegranate seeds. Serve the salad with the feta.

Tomatoes would be my desert island vegetable. Supper rarely seems complete without a plate of sliced beauties on the table, which need be afforded no more than salt, black pepper and sugar to bring out their sweet sourness, and possibly a little extra virgin olive oil or a few slivers of spring onion. But any other takes are welcome, and this has the exotic edge over anything obviously Italianate, its flavouring taking its cue from zaatar, a Lebanese blend of ground sumac and thyme.

tomato salad with thyme and sesame

15g sesame seeds
a small handful of fresh thyme sprigs
2 large or 3 small beefsteak
  tomatoes, core removed and
  thickly sliced
sea salt
4 tablespoons extra virgin olive oil
1 tablespoon lemon juice

Serves 4

Preheat the oven to 180°C fan/200°C/gas mark 6. Scatter the sesame seeds over half a baking tray in a thin layer, and place the thyme sprigs alongside, separating out the sprigs. Toast these in the oven for 12–15 minutes, until the seeds are lightly coloured and the thyme leaves have dried out, then remove and leave to cool.

Arrange the sliced tomatoes on a large plate and season with salt. Remove the thyme leaves by running the twigs between your thumb and first finger. Mix these with the sesame seeds and scatter them over the tomatoes. Pour over the olive oil and then the lemon juice and serve.

In essence this is a tomato salad, one to embark on in the summer months when you can rely on the fruits exuding the necessary juices to soak the bread. It's also wonderfully cooling, a good one for eating in the shade of a big old tree in the garden when the sun is at its highest. Vegetarians needn't miss out – simply omit the anchovies.

panzanella

3 yellow peppers, core and seeds
   removed, cut into thin strips
extra virgin olive oil
sea salt, black pepper
500g cherry or baby plum
   tomatoes, halved
½ teaspoon caster sugar
1 tablespoon red wine vinegar
¾ ciabatta loaf, crusts
   removed, torn into 1–2cm
   chunks
8 anchovies in oil, cut in
   half lengthwise
2 tablespoons capers, rinsed
100g green and black olives,
   pitted and halved
a handful of fresh basil leaves,
   torn in half

Serves 4

Preheat the oven to 180°C fan/200°C/gas mark 6. Arrange the peppers in a roasting dish in a crowded layer, drizzle over 2 tablespoons of olive oil and season them. Roast for 40–45 minutes until caramelised at the edges, stirring halfway through. Remove and leave to cool in the dish.

At the same time, place the tomatoes in a large bowl, toss with 1 level teaspoon of salt and the sugar and set aside for 30 minutes. Drain the tomatoes into a sieve, collecting the juice in a bowl below. Add 6 tablespoons of oil and the vinegar to the juices. Place the bread in a large bowl, sprinkle over the dressing and set aside until it has been absorbed.

Toss the tomatoes, peppers and bread with the anchovies, capers, olives and basil in a large bowl. Cover with cling film and set aside for about 1 hour for the bread to soften further, then give the salad a stir. The salad will be good for some hours. Drizzle over another 2 tablespoons of oil just before serving.

With ingredients as vibrant as this, there's no point in doing anything too complicated — let them shine in a really simple fresh salad. But buffalo mozzarella it has to be (as opposed to a cow's milk usurper), dripping in lovely buttermilk when you slice into it.

mozzarella, pea and mint salad

5 tablespoons extra virgin olive oil
sea salt
caster sugar
200g shelled fresh peas
100g mangetouts, stalk ends trimmed
200g sugar-snaps, stalk ends trimmed
200g buffalo mozzarella
a handful of fresh mint leaves, torn
1 tablespoon lemon juice

Serves 4

Bring 4 tablespoons of water, 1 tablespoon of the olive oil, and half a teaspoon each of salt and sugar to the boil in a medium-size saucepan. Add the peas, and cook over a high heat, tossing almost constantly, for 2–3 minutes or until just tender. Leave them to cool in the liquid.

Bring a large pan of salted water to the boil. Add the mangetouts and sugar-snaps and cook for 2 minutes, then drain them into a colander and briefly run cold water through them. Set aside to cool.

To assemble the salad, drain the peas and combine with the mangetouts and sugar-snaps in a large bowl or on a serving plate. Tear up the mozzarella using your fingers and gently mix into the salad with the mint leaves. Pour over the remaining 4 tablespoons of olive oil and the lemon juice and scatter over some salt. The salad will be good for about an hour; if you want to make it in advance of this, toss in the mint, pour over the lemon juice and season at the last minute.

A mixture of beans – fine green ones, broad beans and mealy cannellini, with feisty little bursts of lemon and capers, and chillies for those that like to up the heat. Time pending, broad beans are nicest skinned, particularly if they are large; a good one to delegate.

big bean salad with lots of lemon

400g fine green beans, stalk ends
   trimmed, halved
200g broad beans, fresh or frozen
1 x 300g tin of cannellini beans,
   drained and rinsed
6 tablespoons extra virgin olive oil
2 lemons, plus 1 tablespoon juice
sea salt
4 tablespoons chopped fresh dill
2 tablespoons small capers, rinsed
75g mild pickled green chillies
   (optional)

Serves 6

Bring two large pans of water to the boil. Add the green beans to one pan and cook for 4–5 minutes, until just tender, then drain into a colander, briefly run under the cold tap and leave to cool. Add the broad beans to the other pan, bring back to the boil and cook for 6–7 minutes if fresh, and 4–5 minutes if frozen. Drain into a colander or sieve, then return to the pan, fill with cold water and leave to cool.

Combine the green beans, broad beans and cannellini beans in a large bowl. Dress with the olive oil, the tablespoon of lemon juice and season with salt. Stir in the dill and capers, and the chillies if including. Cut the skin and white pith off the lemons, quarter them downwards and thinly slice into small wedges. Gently fold these into the salad. It can be made up to an hour in advance, but after this the beans will begin to discolour, though it will still taste good.

Watermelon is only slightly sweeter than cucumber, and makes great salad material offset by a salty cheese — Ossau-Iraty and pecorino would also be good. And a little honey just brings it all together nicely.

salad of watermelon, parsley and manchego

50g pumpkin seeds
300g watermelon, cut into thin wedges 3–4 cm wide, seeds discarded
200g Manchego, cut into thin wedges 3–4 cm wide
4 large handfuls of fresh flat-leaf parsley leaves

3 tablespoons extra virgin olive oil
1 teaspoon runny honey
a squeeze of lemon juice
sea salt

Serves 4–6

Preheat the oven to 180°C fan/200°C/gas mark 6. Scatter the pumpkin seeds over the base of a small baking dish, toast in the oven for 8–10 minutes until lightly coloured, then leave to cool.

Arrange the watermelon, Manchego and parsley in a shallow dish. You can prepare the salad to this point up to a couple of hours in advance, in which case set aside somewhere cool. Just before serving, drizzle over the oil and the honey. Squeeze over a little lemon juice and scrunch over a smattering of salt, then scatter with the pumpkin seeds.

Suppers of seared beef and lamb, not least those cooked on the barbecue, don't have to drag tatties in their wake – a big couscous salad is that much more relaxed. The couscous here is a little drier than if it was destined for a stew, and combined with masses of chopped herbs it is also less stodgy than the norm.

herbed couscous salad

200g couscous
sea salt, black pepper
6 tablespoons extra virgin olive oil
150g fresh herb leaves (including fine stalks), a mixture of rocket, flat-leaf parsley and coriander
3 tomatoes, sliced and then chopped
2 large spring onions, trimmed and finely sliced and then chopped
3 tablespoons lemon juice

Serves 6

Place the couscous in a small saucepan with 300ml of water, half a teaspoon of salt and 1 tablespoon of olive oil. Bring to the boil and let it seethe for 1 minute; you won't actually be able to see it simmering but you'll be able to hear it. Turn the heat off, cover with a lid and leave for 20 minutes before fluffing it up with a fork. Leave it to cool.

Coarsely chop the herbs and combine with the tomato and onion in a large bowl. Add some seasoning, the remaining oil and lemon juice and combine. Finally toss in the couscous. The salad is best served freshly made, ideally within 30 minutes, though you can always assemble it in advance and dress it at the last minute.

Deliciously French and rustic, full of ingredients they excel at producing. It has a really wholesome quality, with the roughly torn, crisp croûtons and salty lardons, and those elegant skinny green beans.

green bean, lardon and country croûton salad

3–4 thick slices of sourdough or
   country bread, crusts removed
1 tablespoon fresh thyme leaves
extra virgin olive oil
400g fine green beans, stalk
   ends trimmed
200g unsmoked lardons or diced
   streaky bacon
1 tablespoon red wine vinegar
1 teaspoon Dijon mustard
sea salt, black pepper
250g small vine tomatoes, quartered
4 tablespoons coarsely chopped fresh
   flat-leaf parsley

Serves 4

Preheat the oven to 220°C fan/240°C/gas mark 9. Lay the slices of bread out on a baking tray, scatter with half the thyme, drizzle over some olive oil and toast in the oven for 9–10 minutes. Turn the bread over and scatter over the rest of the thyme – some of the oil should have seeped through, but give them another light drizzle and cook for a further 9–10 minutes, until golden at the edges and crisp. Leave to cool, then tear into roughly shaped croûtons.

Bring a large pan of salted water to the boil. Add the beans and cook for 3–5 minutes or until tender, then drain them into a colander, briefly run cold water through them and leave to cool.

Heat a large frying pan over a medium heat, add the lardons or bacon and fry in the rendered fat for 9–11 minutes until golden and crisp, stirring occasionally. Drain them on a double thickness of kitchen paper and leave to cool.

To make the dressing, whisk the vinegar with the mustard and some seasoning in a bowl, then gradually whisk in 5 tablespoons of oil – at the end you should have a thick creamy emulsion.

Just before serving toss the beans, tomatoes, lardons and croûtons in a large salad bowl. Pour over the dressing, toss, and mix in the parsley.

This pasta salad is lifted by lots of sweet roasted onions, chopped parsley and olives, not to mention the cherry tomatoes. And layering it in this fashion means you can avoid the stodgy fate of so many salads of this ilk, and even make it in advance.

a layered pasta salad

2 red onions, peeled, halved and thinly
  sliced
1 teaspoon fresh thyme leaves
extra virgin olive oil
sea salt, black pepper
150g conchiglie
400g baby plum tomatoes, halved
7 tablespoons coarsely chopped fresh
  flat-leaf parsley
125g green and black olives, pitted
1 tablespoon balsamic vinegar

Serves 4

Preheat the oven to 200°C fan/220°C/gas mark 7. Arrange the onion slices in a single layer in a shallow roasting dish, scatter over the thyme, drizzle over a little oil, season and roast for 20 minutes, then leave to cool.

In the meantime, bring a large pan of salted water to the boil. Add the pasta, give it a stir and cook for 10–12 minutes, until just tender, or as indicated on the pack. Drain it into a sieve, run cold water through it, then return it to the pan and toss with a tablespoon of oil.

Place the tomatoes in the bottom of a large deep salad bowl and season them with salt and pepper. Scatter the parsley over, then the pasta, the onions and finally the olives. Cover with cling film and set aside in a cool place.

Whisk the balsamic vinegar with 6 tablespoons of olive oil. At the table, pour the dressing over the salad and toss before serving.

With its Spanish tones, the hankering here is for a glass of fino and a little seafood alongside. A nice piece of grilled fish, a few shell-on prawns, some mussels in their shells or some such. Unless your new potatoes are genuine earlies and can be scrubbed of most of their papery skins, they will need peeling.

new potatoes with garlic yoghurt

1 head of garlic, cloves separated
    and peeled
2 bay leaves
3 tablespoons extra virgin olive oil
sea salt
750g new potatoes, scrubbed
    and halved if large

250g Greek yoghurt
a squeeze of lemon juice
paprika to serve

Serves 4–6

Place the garlic, bay leaves, olive oil, 500ml of water and a little salt in a large saucepan. Bring to the boil, then add the potatoes, bring back to the boil, cover and simmer for 15 minutes or until the potatoes are tender when pierced with a knife. Transfer the potatoes to a bowl to cool, using a slotted spoon, leaving the garlic and bay leaves in the liquor. Turn the heat up, bring back to the boil and cook to reduce to a few tablespoons of liquid. Using a potato masher, mash the garlic into the juices. Transfer to a bowl and leave to cool, then whisk this into the yoghurt with a squeeze of lemon juice. Taste for seasoning and add a little more salt if necessary.

Once the potatoes are cool, slice and arrange them in a large bowl. Spoon the sauce over and sprinkle with paprika.

get dressed

A good repertoire of dressings is almost more important come suppertime than whatever material you have in the salad drawer. It is this that will serve to inspire and bring everything to life, whether it's a really good vinaigrette (essential for any selection of green leaves), a thick yellow Heinz-style salad cream, or a walnut cream.

Serves 6

house vinaigrette

This is my stock dressing that I make in quantity in a
Le Parfait jar, so putting a green salad on the table means
no more than preparing the leaves at the time.

1 tablespoon red wine vinegar
1 teaspoon Dijon mustard
1 garlic clove, peeled and crushed to a paste
1 teaspoon golden caster sugar
sea salt, black pepper
5 tablespoons groundnut oil
2 tablespoons extra virgin olive oil

Whisk the vinegar, mustard, garlic, sugar and some seasoning
in a bowl, then whisk in the oils.

french walnut cream

A great one for a big bowl of lamb's lettuce, especially with
crisp lardons and walnuts.

75g crème fraîche or sour cream
1 tablespoon walnut oil
½ teaspoon Dijon mustard
a few drops of cider vinegar
sea salt, black pepper

Whisk the crème fraîche with the walnut oil, mustard, cider
vinegar and a little seasoning in a small bowl.

a little lemon dressing

Try this with a bowl of rocket and slivers of Parmesan.

1 tablespoon lemon juice
¼ teaspoon finely grated lemon zest
sea salt, black pepper
4 tablespoons extra virgin olive oil

Whisk the lemon juice and zest with some seasoning in a
bowl, then add the oil.

very heinz salad cream

Keep the English credentials of the salad ingredients close to
your heart – floppy green lettuces, breakfast radishes, spring
onions, quarters of egg and snipped chives. It's great over cold
boiled potatoes too.

3 medium organic egg yolks
4 tablespoons double cream
1 teaspoon English mustard
1 teaspoon caster sugar
1 tablespoon white wine vinegar
sea salt

Whisk all the ingredients for the dressing in a bowl set over
a pan with a little simmering water in it, then stir constantly
for a few minutes until it thickens, taking care not to overheat
otherwise it will scramble. Pass the salad cream through a
sieve into a bowl, cover the surface with cling film and leave
to cool, then chill until required. You can also make it in
quantity in advance, and it will keep well in the fridge for a
week providing the cream is fresh.

endings six notes to end on

raspberries and clotted cream

Raspberries are a fruit we grow beautifully in this country – soft perfumed berries, as sweet as they are sour, which is always a guarantee of intensity. They actually deserve that spoon of clotted cream; but rather than dish it up yourself, give everyone the pleasure of diving down through the buttery yellow crust to the sticky liquid cream below the surface and the curdy cream below that. Or take it one step further and provide a pile of lily-white meringues. Place all three centrally so everyone can help themselves and mash them together into an Eton Mess.

valrhona and muscatel raisins

Valrhona no longer have the monopoly on gorgeous dark chocolate, but they do make the biggest bars. The ideal here is one so large that you have to splinter it with a large cook's knife, and some juicy sweet muscatel raisins on the vine to partner the shavings.

dates and fresh goat's cheese

It's those intensely sweet fudgy Medjool dates I had in mind here, perfectly matched by a faintly salty fresh young goat's cheese, though mascarpone and ricotta will also do it. I'd put a jar of flower-scented honey and a dipper on the table at the ready too.

walnuts and blue cheese

When I am in France I miss Stilton, and when I am in England I miss Roquefort. These for me are the two great 'blues' that cannot be bettered than when served with some walnuts to crack. Though you could also try mashing a little of the cheese with a slug of sherry, and provide morsels of raisin or nut bread to scoop it up.

vacherin mont d'or and chicory

Whenever you eat a semi-soft cheese and wish that it consisted entirely of the perfectly runny bit just below the rind, you are dreaming of vacherin Mont d'Or. Of all cheeses, this has to be the most indulgent and luxurious, silken goo headily scented with the spruce bark that surrounds it; you're instantly transported to the fireside of a log cabin in some far-off winter wonderland. But make the most of it when you see it, as the season doesn't last long – it's a late autumn and winter treat. Crisp leaves of chicory strike just the right insouciant note.

pink champagne and biscuits de reims

When the French give you a bottle of Champagne, it is usually accompanied by a packet of sponge fingers or savoiardi. But in Reims, the Champagne capital, they go one step further than this with biscuits de Reims, little hardened pale pink biscuits designed specifically with the wine of the region in mind, for dunking. When it comes to pud, pink fizz is even more of a treat than blonde, and even matches the biscuits. Cantuccini and sweet wine are in the same vein, a small glass of syrupy sweet wine with a baked-hard biscuit to soak it up.

index

acknowledgements

With many thanks to Angela Mason, Food Editor on YOU Magazine, to Sue Peart, Editor, and John Koski, Associated Editor. Also to my agent Rosemary Sandberg, to

Suzanna de Jong, Editor, Annie Lee, Copy Editor, and to Kyle Cathie. And with love and thanks to Jonnie, Rothko and Louis.